LITTLE FOXES

LITTLE FOXES

OR

THE INSIGNIFICANT LITTLE HABITS WHICH MAR DOMESTIC HAPPINESS.

MRS. HARRIET BEECHER STOWE.

GYAN

Published by

Gyan Publishing House
5, Ansari Road
Daryaganj, New Delhi-110002
Phone: 011-47034999, 9811692060
E-mail: books@gyanbooks.com

Distribution Network
gyanbooks.com
India, USA, Canada, UK, Australia, France

ISBN : 978-81-212-9528-4 (PB)
First Published, 1866

2nd Impression 2023

Printed at: Gyan Press, Delhi.

LITTLE FOXES
Author: MRS. HARRIET BEECHER STOWE.

LITTLE FOXES.

LITTLE FOXES;

OR,

THE INSIGNIFICANT *LITTLE* HABITS WHICH MAR DOMESTIC HAPPINESS.

BY

MRS. HARRIET BEECHER STOWE.

[*AUTHOR'S EDITION, REVISED.*]

1866.

PREFATORY NOTICE.

From a desire to respect the moral right of every Author to reap the fruits of his or her pen, the Publishers have made arrangements to share the profits of this reprint of "Little Foxes" with the Writer.

CONTENTS.

LITTLE FOXES.

INTRODUCTION.

"PAPA, what are you going to give us this winter for our evening readings?" said Jennie.

"I am thinking, for one thing," I replied, "of preaching a course of household sermons from a very odd text prefixed to a discourse which I found at the bottom of the pamphlet-barrel in the garret."

"Don't say sermon, papa,—it has such a dreadful sound; and on winter evenings one wants something entertaining."

"Well, treatise, then," said I, "or discourse, or essay, or prelection; I'm not particular as to words."

"But what is the queer text that you found at the bottom of the pamphlet-barrel?"

"It was one preached upon by your mother's great-great-grandfather, the very savory and much-respected Simeon Shuttleworth, 'on the occasion of the melancholy defections and divisions among the godly in the town of West Dofield;' and it runs thus,—'*Take us the foxes, the little foxes, that spoil the vines: for our vines have tender grapes.'*"

"It's a curious text enough; but I can't imagine what you are going to make of it."

"Simply an essay on Little Foxes," said I; "by which I mean those unsuspected, unwatched, insignificant *little* causes that nibble away domestic happiness, and make home less than so noble an institution should be. You may build beautiful, convenient, attractive houses,—you may hang the walls with lovely pictures and stud them with gems of Art; and there may be living there together persons bound by blood and affection in one common interest, leading a life common to themselves and apart from others; and these persons may each one of them be possessed of good and noble traits; there may be a common basis of affection, of generosity, of good principle, of religion; and yet, through the influence of some of these perverse, nibbling, insignificant little foxes, half the clusters of happiness on these so promising vines may fail to come to maturity. A little community of people, all of whom would be willing to die for each other, may not be able to live happily together; that is, they may have far less happiness than their circumstances, their fine and excellent traits, entitle them to expect.

The reason for this in general is that home is a place not only of strong affections, but of entire unreserve; it is life's undress rehearsal, its back-room, its dressing-room, from which we go forth to more careful and guarded intercourse, leaving behind us much *débris* of cast-off and every-day clothing. Hence has arisen the common proverb, 'No man is a hero to his *valet-de-chambre;*' and the common warning, 'If you wish to keep your friend, don't go and live with him.'"

"Which is only another way of saying," said my wife, "that we are all human and imperfect; and the nearer you get to any human being, the more defects you see. The characters that can stand the test of daily intimacy are about as numerous as four-leaved clovers in a meadow; in general, those who do not annoy you with positive faults bore you with their insipidity. The evenness and beauty of a strong, well-defined nature, perfectly governed and balanced, is about the last thing one is likely to meet with in one's researches into life."

"But what I have to say," replied I, "is this,—that, family-life being a state of unreserve, a state in which there are few of those barriers and veils that keep people in the world from seeing each other's defects and mutually jarring and grating upon each other, it is remarkable that it is entered upon and maintained generally with less reflection, less care and forethought, than pertain to most kinds of business which men and women set their hands to. A man does not undertake to run an engine or manage a piece of machinery without some careful examination of its parts and capabilities, and some inquiry whether he have the necessary knowledge, skill, and strength to make it do itself and him justice. A man does not try to play on the violin without seeing whether his fingers are long and flexible enough to bring out the harmonies and raise his performance above the grade of dismal scraping to that of divine music. What should we think of a man who should set a whole orchestra of instruments upon playing together without the least provision or forethought as to their chording, and then howl and tear his hair at the result? It is not the fault of the instruments that they grate harsh thunders together; they may each be noble and of celestial temper; but united without regard to their nature, dire confusion is the result. Still worse were it, if a man were supposed so stupid as to expect of each instrument a *rôle* opposed to its nature,—if he asked of the octave-flute a bass solo, and condemned the trombone because it could not do the work of the many-voiced violin.

"Yet just so carelessly is the work of forming a family often performed. A man and woman come together from some affinity, some partial accord of their nature which has inspired mutual affection. There is generally very little careful consideration of who and what they are,—no thought of the reciprocal influence of mutual traits,—no previous chording and testing of the instruments which are to make lifelong harmony or discord,—and after a short period of engagement, in which all their mutual relations are made as opposite as possible to those which must follow marriage, these two furnish their house and begin life together. Ten to one, the domestic roof is supposed at once the proper refuge for relations and friends on both sides, who also are introduced into the interior concert without any special consideration of what is likely to be the operation of character on character, the play of instrument with instrument; then follow children, each of whom is a separate entity, a separate will, a separate force in the family; and thus, with the lesser forces of servants and dependents, a family is made up. And there is no wonder if all these chance-assorted instruments, playing together, sometimes make quite as much discord as harmony. For if the husband and wife chord, the wife's sister or husband's mother may introduce a discord; and then again, each child of marked character introduces another possibility of confusion. The conservative forces of human nature are so strong and so various, that, with all these drawbacks, the family state is after all the best and purest happiness that earth affords. But then, with cultivation and care, it might be a great deal happier. Very fair pears have been raised by dropping a seed into a good soil and letting it alone for years; but finer and choicer are raised by the watchings, tendings, prunings of the gardener. Wild grape-vines bore very fine grapes, and an abundance of them, before our friend Dr. Grant took up his abode at Iona, and, studying the laws of Nature, conjured up new species of rarer fruit and flavour out of the old. And so, if all the little foxes that infest our domestic vine and fig-tree were once hunted out and killed, we might have fairer clusters and fruit all winter."

"But, papa," said Jennie, "to come to the foxes; let's know what they are."

"Well, as the text says, they are *little* foxes, the pet foxes of good people, unsuspected little animals,—on the whole, often thought to be really creditable little beasts, that may do good, and at all events cannot do much harm. And as I have taken to the Puritanic order in my discourse, I shall set them in sevens, as Noah did his clean beasts in the ark. Now my seven little foxes are these:—

1. Fault-finding.
2. Irritability.
3. Repression.
4. Self-will.
5. Intolerance.
6. Discourteousness.
7. Exactingness.

"And here," turning to my sermon, "is what I have to say about the first of them."

I.

FAULT-FINDING.

A MOST respectable little animal, that many people let run freely among their domestic vines, under the notion that he helps the growth of the grapes, and is the principal means of keeping them in order.

Now it may safely be set down as a maxim, that nobody likes to be found fault with, but everybody likes to find fault when things do not suit him.

Let my courteous reader ask him or herself if he or she does not experience a relief and pleasure in finding fault with or about whatever troubles them.

This appears at first sight an anomaly in the provisions of Nature. Generally we are so constituted, that what it is a pleasure to us to do, it is a pleasure to our neighbour to have us do. It is a pleasure to give, and a pleasure to receive. It is a pleasure to love, and a pleasure to be loved; a pleasure to admire, a pleasure to be admired. It is a pleasure also to find fault, but *not* a pleasure to be found fault with. Furthermore, those people whose sensitiveness of temperament leads them to find the most fault, are precisely those who can least bear to be found fault with; they bind heavy burdens and grievous to be borne, and lay them on other men's shoulders, but they themselves cannot bear the weight of a finger.

Now the difficulty in the case is this: There are things in life that need to be altered; and that things may be altered, they must be spoken of to the people whose business it is to make the change. This opens wide the door of fault-finding to well-disposed people, and gives them latitude of conscience to impose on their fellows all the annoyances which they themselves feel. The father and mother of a family are fault-finders, *ex officio*; and to them flows back the tide of every separate individual's complaints in the domestic circle, till often the whole air of the house is chilled and darkened by a drizzling Scotch mist of querulousness. Very bad are these mists for grape-vines, and produce mildew in many a fair cluster.

Enthusius falls in love with Hermione, because she looks like a moonbeam,—because she is ethereal as a summer cloud, *spirituelle*. He commences forthwith the perpetual adoration system that precedes marriage. He assures her that she is too good for this world, too delicate and fair for any of the uses of poor mortality,—that she ought to tread on roses, sleep on the clouds,—that she ought never to shed a tear, know a fatigue, or make an exertion, but live apart in some bright, ethereal sphere worthy of her charms. All which is duly chanted in her ear in moonlight walks or sails, and so often repeated that a sensible girl may be excused for believing that a little of it may be true.

Now comes marriage,—and it turns out that Enthusius is very particular as to his coffee, that he is excessively disturbed if his meals are at all irregular, and that he cannot be comfortable with any table arrangements which do not resemble those of his notable mother, lately deceased in the odour of sanctity; he also wants his house in perfect order at all hours. Still he does not propose to provide a trained housekeeper; it is all to be effected by means of certain raw Irish girls, under the superintendence of this angel who was to tread on roses, sleep on clouds, and never know an earthly care. Neither has Enthusius ever considered it a part of a husband's duty to bear personal inconveniences in silence. He would freely shed his blood for Hermione,—nay, has often frantically proposed the same in the hours of courtship, when of course nobody wanted it done, and it could answer no manner of use; and thus to the idyllic dialogues of that period succeed such as these:—

"My dear, this tea is smoked: can't you get Jane into the way of making it better?"

"My dear, I have tried; but she will not do as I tell her."

"Well, all I know is, other people can have good tea, and I should think we might."

And again at dinner:—

"My dear, this mutton is overdone again; it is *always* overdone."

"Not always, dear, because you recollect on Monday you said it was just right."

"Well, *almost* always."

"Well, my dear, the reason to-day was, I had company in the parlour, and could not go out to caution Bridget, as I generally do. It's very difficult to get things done with such a girl."

"My mother's things were always well done, no matter what her girl was."

Again: "My dear, you must speak to the servants about wasting the coal. I never saw such a consumption of fuel in a family of our size;" or, "My dear, how can you let Maggie tear the morning paper?" or, "My dear, I shall actually have to give up coming to dinner if my dinners cannot be regular;" or, "My dear, I wish you would look at the way my shirts are ironed,—it is perfectly scandalous;" or, "My dear, you must not let Johnnie finger the mirror in the parlour;" or, "My dear, you must stop the children from playing in the garret;" or, "My dear, you must see that Maggie doesn't leave the mat out on the railing when she sweeps the front hall;" and so on, up-stairs and down-stairs, in the lady's chamber, in attic, garret, and cellar, "my dear" is to see that nothing goes wrong, and she is found fault with when anything does.

Yet Enthusius, when occasionally he finds his sometime angel in tears, and she tells him he does not love her as he once did, repudiates the charge with all his heart, and declares he loves her more than ever,—and perhaps he does. The only thing is that she has passed out of the plane of moonshine and poetry into that of actualities. While she was considered an angel, a star, a bird, an evening cloud, of course there was nothing to be found fault with in her; but now that the angel has become chief business-partner in an earthly working firm, relations are different. Enthusius could say the same things over again under the same circumstances, but unfortunately now they never are in the same circumstances. Enthusius is simply a man who is in the habit of speaking from impulse, and saying a thing merely and only because he feels it. Before marriage he worshipped and adored his wife as an ideal being dwelling in the land of dreams and poetries, and did his very best to make her unpractical and unfitted to enjoy the life to which he was to introduce her after marriage. After marriage he still yields unreflectingly to present impulses, which are no longer to praise, but to criticize and condemn. The very sensibility to beauty and love of elegance, which made him admire her before marriage, now transferred to the arrangement of the domestic *ménage*, lead him daily to perceive a hundred defects and find a hundred annoyances.

Thus far we suppose an amiable, submissive wife, who is only grieved, not provoked,—who has no sense of injustice, and meekly strives to make good the hard conditions of her lot. Such poor, little, faded women have we seen, looking for all the world like plants that have been nursed and forced into bloom in the steam-heat of the conservatory, and are now sickly and yellow, dropping leaf by leaf, in the dry, dusty parlour.

But there is another side of the picture,—where the wife, provoked and indignant, takes up the fault-finding trade in return, and with the keen arrows of her woman's wit, searches and penetrates every joint of the husband's armour, showing herself full as unjust and far more culpable in this sort of conflict.

Saddest of all sad things is it to see two once very dear friends employing all that peculiar knowledge of each other which love had given them only to harass and provoke,—thrusting and piercing with a certainty of aim that only past habits of confidence and affection could have put in their power, wounding their own hearts with every deadly thrust they made at one another, and all for such inexpressibly miserable trifles as usually form the openings of fault-finding dramas.

For the contentions that loosen the very foundations of love, that crumble away all its fine traceries and carved work, about what miserable worthless things do they commonly begin!—a dinner underdone, too much oil consumed, a newspaper torn, a waste of coal or soap, a dish broken!—and for this miserable sort of trash, very good, very generous, very religious people will sometimes waste and throw away by double-handfuls the very thing for which houses are built, and coal burned, and all the paraphernalia of a home established, —*their happiness.* Better cold coffee, smoky tea, burnt meat, better any inconvenience, any loss, than a loss of *love;* and nothing so surely burns away love as constant fault-finding.

For fault-finding once allowed as a habit between two near and dear friends comes in time to establish a chronic soreness, so that the mildest, the most reasonable suggestion, the gentlest implied reproof, occasions burning irritation; and when this morbid state has once set in, the restoration of love seems well nigh impossible.

For example: Enthusius having got up this morning in the best of humours, in the most playful tones begs Hermione not to make the tails of her *g's* quite so long; and Hermione fires up with—

"And, pray, what else wouldn't you wish me to do? Perhaps you would be so good, when you have leisure, as to make out an alphabetical list of the things in me that need correcting."

"My dear, you are unreasonable."

"I don't think so. I should like to get to the end of the requirements of my lord and master sometimes."

"Now, my dear, you really are very silly."

"Please say something original, my dear. I have heard that till it has lost the charm of novelty."

"Come now, Hermione, don't let's quarrel."

"My dear sir, who thinks of quarrelling? Not I; I'm sure I was only asking to be directed. I trust some time, if I live to be ninety, to suit your fastidious taste. I trust the coffee is right this morning, *and* the tea, *and* the toast, *and* the steak, *and* the servants, *and* the front-hall mat, *and* the upper-story hall door, *and* the basement premises; and now I suppose I am to be trained in respect to my general education. I shall set about the tails of my *g's* at once, but trust you will prepare a list of any other little things that need emendation."

Enthusius pushes away his coffee, and drums on the table.

"If I might be allowed one small criticism, my dear,

I should observe that it is not good manners to drum on the table," said his fair opposite.

"Hermione, you are enough to drive a man frantic!" exclaims Enthusius, rushing out with bitterness in his soul, and a determination to take his dinner at Delmonico's.

Enthusius feels himself an abused man, and thinks there never was such a sprite of a woman,—the most utterly unreasonable, provoking human being he ever met with. What he does not think of is, that it is his own inconsiderate, constant fault-finding that has made every nerve so sensitive and sore, that the mildest suggestion of advice or reproof on the most indifferent subject is impossible. He has not, to be sure, been the guilty partner in this morning's encounter; he has said only what is fair and proper, and she has been unreasonable and cross; but, after all, the fault is remotely his.

When Enthusius awoke, after marriage, to find in his Hermione in very deed only a bird, a star, a flower, but no housekeeper, why did he not face the matter like an honest man? Why did he not remember all the fine things about dependence and uselessness with which he had been filling her head for a year or two, and in common honesty exact no more from her than he had bargained for? Can a bird make a good business manager? Can a flower oversee Biddy and Mike, and impart to their uncircumcised ears the high crafts and mysteries of elegant housekeeping?

If his little wife has to learn her domestic *rôle* of

household duty, as most girls do, by a thousand mortifications, a thousand perplexities, a thousand failures, let him, in ordinary fairness, make it as easy to her as possible. Let him remember with what admiring smiles, before marriage, he received her pretty professions of utter helplessness and incapacity in domestic matters, finding only poetry and grace in what, after marriage, proved an annoyance.

And if a man finds that he has a wife ill-adapted to wifely duties, does it follow that the best thing he can do is to blurt out, without form or ceremony, all the criticisms and corrections which may occur to him in the many details of household life? He would not dare to speak with as little preface, apology, or circumlocution, to his business manager, to his butcher, or his baker. When Enthusius was a bachelor, he never criticised the table at his boarding-house without some reflection, and studying to take unto himself acceptable words whereby to soften the asperity of the criticism. The laws of society require that a man should qualify, soften, and wisely time his admonitions to those he meets in the outer world, or they will turn again and rend him. But to his own wife, in his own house and home, he can find fault without ceremony or softening. So he can; and he can awake, in the course of a year or two, to find his wife a changed woman, and his home unendurable. He may find, too, that unceremonious fault-finding is a game that two can play at, and that a woman can shoot her arrows with far more precision and skill than a man.

But the fault lies not always on the side of the husband. Quite as often is a devoted, patient, good-tempered man harassed and hunted and baited by the inconsiderate fault-finding of a wife whose principal talent seems to lie in the ability at first glance to discover and make manifest the weak point in everything.

We have seen the most generous, the most warm-hearted and obliging of mortals, under this sort of training, made the most morose and disobliging of husbands. Sure to be found fault with, whatever they do, they have at last ceased doing. The disappointment of not pleasing they have abated by not trying to please.

We once knew a man who married a spoiled beauty, whose murmurs, exactions, and caprices were infinite. He had at last, as a refuge to his wearied nerves, settled down into a habit of utter disregard and neglect; he treated her wishes and her complaints with equal indifference, and went on with his life as nearly as possible as if she did not exist. He silently provided for her what he thought proper, without troubling himself to notice her requests or listen to her grievances. Sickness came, but the heart of her husband was cold and gone; there was no sympathy left to warm her. Death came, and he breathed freely as a man released. He married again,—a woman with no beauty, but much love and goodness,—a woman who asked little, blamed seldom, and then with all the tact and address which the utmost thoughtfulness could devise; and the passive, negligent husband became the attentive, devoted slave of her will. He was in her hands as clay in the hands of the potter; the least breath or suggestion of criticism from her lips, who criticised so little and so thoughtfully, weighed more with him than many outspoken words. So different is the same human being, according to the touch of the hand which plays upon him!

I have spoken hitherto of fault-finding as between husband and wife: its consequences are even worse as respects children. The habit once suffered to grow up between the two that constitute the head of the family descends and runs through all the branches. Children are more hurt by indiscriminate, thoughtless fault-finding than by any other one thing. Often a child has all the sensitiveness and all the susceptibility of a grown person, added to the faults of childhood. Nothing about him is right as yet; he is immature and faulty at all points, and everybody feels at perfect liberty to criticize him to right and left, above, below, and around, till he takes refuge either in callous hardness or irritable moroseness.

A bright, noisy boy rushes in from school, eager to tell his mother something he has on his heart, and Number One cries out,—

"Oh, you've left the door open! I do wish you wouldn't always leave the door open! And do look at the mud on your shoes! How many times must I tell you to wipe your feet?"

"Now there you've thrown your cap on the sofa again! When will you learn to hang it up?"

"Don't put your slate there; that isn't the place for it."

"How dirty your hands are! what have you been doing?"

"Don't sit in that chair; you break the springs, jouncing."

"Mercy! how your hair looks! Do go up-stairs and comb it."

"There, if you haven't torn the braid all off your coat! Dear me, what a boy!"

"Don't speak so loud; your voice goes through my head."

"I want to know, Jim, if it was you that broke up that barrel that I have been saving for brown flour."

"I believe it was you, Jim, that hacked the edge of my razor."

"Jim's been writing at my desk, and blotted three sheets of the best paper."

Now the question is, if any of the grown people of the family had to run the gauntlet of a string of criticisms on themselves equally true as those that salute unlucky Jim, would they be any better-natured about it than he is?

No; but they are grown-up people; they have rights that others are bound to respect. Everybody cannot tell them exactly what he thinks about everything they do. If every one could and did, would there not be terrible reactions?

Servants in general are only grown-up children, and the same considerations apply to them. A raw, untrained Irish girl introduced into an elegant house has her head bewildered in every direction. There are the gas-pipes, the water-pipes, the whole paraphernalia of elegant and delicate conveniences, about which a thousand little details are to be learned, the neglect of any one of which may flood the house, or poison it with foul air, or bring innumerable inconveniences. The setting of a genteel table and the waiting upon it involve fifty possibilities of mistake, each one of which will grate on the nerves of a whole family. There is no wonder, then, that the occasions of fault-finding in families are so constant and harassing; and there is no wonder that mistress and maid often meet each other on the terms of the bear and the man who fell together fifty feet down from the limb of a high tree, and lay at the bottom of it, looking each other in the face in helpless, growling despair. The mistress is rasped, irritated, despairing, and with good reason; the maid is the same, and with equally good reason. Yet let the mistress be suddenly introduced into a printing-office, and required, with what little teaching could be given her in a few rapid directions, to set up the editorial of a morning paper, and it is probable she would be as stupid and bewildered as Biddy in her beautifully-arranged house.

There are elegant houses which, from causes like these, are ever vexed like the troubled sea that cannot rest. Literally, their table has become a snare before them, and that which should have been for their welfare, a trap. Their gas, and their water, and their fire, and their elegancies and ornaments, all in unskilled, blundering hands, seem only so many guns in the hands of Satan, through which he fires at their Christian graces day and night,—so that, if their house is kept in order, their temper and religion are not.

I am speaking now to the consciousness of thousands of women who are, in will and purpose, real saints. Their souls go up to heaven—its love, its purity, its rest—with every hymn and prayer and sacrament in church; and they come home to be mortified, disgraced, and made to despise themselves, for the unlovely tempers, the hasty words, the cross looks, the universal nervous irritability, that result from this constant jarring of finely toned chords under unskilled hands.

Talk of hair-cloth shirts, and scourgings, and sleeping on ashes, as means of saintship! there is no need of them in our country. Let a woman once look at her domestic trials as her hair-cloth, her ashes, her scourges,—accept them,—rejoice in them,—smile and be quiet, silent, patient, and loving under them,—and the convent can teach her no more; she is a victorious saint.

When the damper of the furnace is turned the wrong way by Paddy, after the five hundredth time of explanation, and the whole family awakes coughing, sneezing, strangling,—when the gas is blown out in the nursery by Biddy, who has been instructed every day for weeks in the danger of such a proceeding,—when the tumblers on the dinner-table are found dim and streaked, after weeks of training in the simple business of washing and wiping,—when the ivory-handled knives and forks are left soaking in hot dish-water, after incessant explanations of the consequences,—when four or five half-civilized beings, above, below, and all over the house, are constantly forgetting the most important things at the very moment it is most necessary they should remember them,—there is no hope for the mistress morally, unless she can in very deed and truth accept her trials religiously, and conquer by accepting. It is not apostles alone who can take pleasure in necessities and distresses; but mothers and housewives also, if they would learn of the apostle, might say, "When I am weak, then am I strong."

The burden ceases to gall when we have learned how to carry it. We can suffer patiently if we see any good come of it, and say, as an old black woman of our acquaintance did, of an event that crossed her purpose, "Well, Lord, if it's *you*, send it along."

But that this may be done, that home life, in our unsettled, changing state of society, may become peaceful and restful, there is one Christian grace, much treated of by mystic writers, that must return to its honour in the Christian Church. I mean—THE GRACE OF SILENCE.

No words can express, no tongue can tell, the value of NOT SPEAKING. "Speech is silvern, but silence is golden," is an old and very precious proverb.

"But," say many voices, "what is to become of us, if we may not speak? Must we not correct our children, and our servants, and each other? Must we let people go on doing wrong to the end of the chapter?"

"No; fault must be found; faults must be told, errors

corrected. Reproof and admonition are duties of householders to their families, and of all true friends to one another.

But, gentle reader, let us look over life, our own lives and the lives of others, and ask, How much of the fault-finding which prevails has the least tendency to do any good? How much of it is well-timed, well-pointed, deliberate, just, and so spoken as to be effective?

"A wise reprover upon an obedient ear," is one of the *rare* things spoken of by Solomon,—the rarest, perhaps, to be met with. How many really religious people put any of their religion into their manner of performing this most difficult office? We find fault with a stove or furnace which creates heat only to go up the chimney and not to warm the house. We say it is wasteful. Just so wasteful often seem prayer-meetings, church-services, and sacraments; they create and excite lovely, gentle, holy feelings,—but, if these do not pass out into the atmosphere of daily life, and warm and clear the air of our homes, there is a great waste in our religion.

We have been on our knees, confessing humbly that we are as awkward in heavenly things, as unfit for the Heavenly Jerusalem, as Biddy and Mike, and the little beggar-girl on our door-steps, are for our parlours. We have deplored our errors daily, hourly, and confessed that "the remembrance of them is grievous unto us, the burden of them is intolerable," and then we draw near in the Sacrament to that Incarnate Divinity whose infinite love covers all our imperfections with the mantle of His perfections. But when we return, do we take our servants and children by the throat because they are as untrained and awkward and careless in earthly things as we have been in heavenly? Does no remembrance of Christ's infinite patience temper our impatience, when we have spoken seventy times seven, and our words have been disregarded? There is no mistake as to the sincerity of the religion which the church excites. What we want is to have it *used* in common life, instead of going up like hot air in a fire-place to lose itself in the infinite abysses above.

In reproving and fault-finding, we have beautiful examples in Holy Writ. When St. Paul has a reproof to administer to delinquent Christians, how does he temper it with gentleness and praise! how does he first make honourable note of all the good there is to be spoken of! how does he give assurance of his prayers and love!—and when at last the arrow flies, it goes all the straighter to the mark for this carefulness.

But there was a greater, a purer, a lovelier than Paul, who made his home on earth, with twelve plain men, ignorant, prejudiced, slow to learn,—and who to the very day of his death were still contending on a point which he had repeatedly explained, and troubling His last earthly hours with the old contest, "Who should be greatest." When all else failed, on His knees before them as their servant, tenderly performing for love the office of a slave, He said, "If I, your Lord and Master, have washed your feet, ye also ought to wash one another's feet."

When parents, employers, and masters learn to reprove in this spirit, reproofs will be more effective than they now are. It was by the exercise of this spirit that Fenélon transformed the proud, petulant, irritable, selfish Duke of Burgundy, making him humble, gentle, tolerant of others and severe only to himself: it was he who had for his motto, that "Perfection alone can bear with imperfection."

But apart from the fault-finding which has a definite aim, how much is there that does not profess or intend or try to do anything more than give vent to an irritated state of feeling! The nettle stings us, and we toss it with both hands at our neighbour; the fire burns us, and we throw coals and hot ashes at all or sundry of those about us.

There is *fretfulness*, a mizzling, drizzling rain of discomforting remark; there is *grumbling*, a north-east storm that never clears: there is *scolding*, the thunder-storm with lightning and hail. All these are worse than useless; they are positive *sins*, by whomsoever indulged,—sins as great and real as many that are shuddered at in polite society.

All these are for the most part but the venting on our fellow-beings of morbid feelings resulting from dyspepsia, overtaxed nerves, or general ill health.

A minister eats too much mince-pie, goes to his weekly lecture, and, seeing only half a dozen people there, proceeds to grumble at those half-dozen for the sins of such as stay away. "The church is cold, there is no interest in religion," and so on: a simple outpouring of the blues.

You and I do in one week the work we ought to do in six; we overtax nerve and brain, and then have weeks of darkness in which everything at home seems running to destruction. The servants never were so careless, the children never so noisy, the house never so disorderly, the State never so ill-governed, the Church evidently going over to Antichrist. The only thing, after all, in which the existing condition of affairs differs from that of a week ago is, that we have used up our nervous energy, and are looking at the world through blue spectacles. We ought to resist the devil of fault-finding at this point, and cultivate silence as a grace till our nerves are rested. There are times when no one should trust himself to judge his neighbours, or reprove his children and servants, or find fault with his friends, —for he is so sharp-set that he cannot strike a note without striking too hard. Then is the time to try the grace of silence, and, what is better than silence, the power of prayer.

But it being premised that we are *never* to fret, never to grumble, never to scold, and yet it being our duty in some way to make known and get rectified the faults of others, it remains to ask how; and on this head we will improvise a parable of two women.

Mrs. Standfast is a woman of high tone, and possessed of a power of moral principle that impresses one even as sublime. All her perceptions of right and wrong are clear, exact, and minute; she is charitable to the poor, kind to the sick and suffering, and devoutly and earnestly religious. In all the minutiæ of woman's life she manifests an inconceivable precision and perfection. Everything she does is perfectly done. She is true to all her promises to the very letter, and so punctual that railroad time might be kept by her instead of a chronometer.

Yet, with all these excellent traits, Mrs. Standfast has not the faculty of making a happy home. She is that most hopeless of fault-finders,—a fault-finder from principle. She has a high correct standard for everything in the world, from the regulation of the thoughts down to the spreading of a sheet or the hemming of a towel; and to this exact standard she feels it her duty to bring every one in her household. She does not often scold, she is not actually fretful, but she exercises over her household a calm, inflexible severity rebuking every fault; she overlooks nothing; she excuses nothing; she will accept of nothing in any part of her domain but absolute perfection; and her reproofs are aimed with a true and steady point, and sent with a force that makes them felt by the most obdurate.

Hence, though she is rarely seen out of temper, and seldom or never scolds, yet she drives every one around her to despair by the use of the calmest and most elegant English. Her servants fear, but do not love her. Her husband—an impulsive, generous man, somewhat inconsiderate and careless in his habits—is at times perfectly desperate under the accumulated load of her disapprobation. Her children regard her as inhabiting some high, distant, unapproachable mountain-top of goodness, whence she is always looking down with reproving eyes on naughty boys and girls. They wonder how it is that so excellent a mamma should have children who, let them try to be good as hard as they can, are always sure to do something dreadful every day.

The trouble with Mrs. Standfast is, not that she has a high standard, and not that she purposes and means to bring every one up to it, but that she does not take the right way. She has set it down that to blame a wrong-doer is the only way to cure wrong. She has never learned that it is as much her duty to praise as to blame, and that people are drawn to do right by being praised when they do it, rather than driven by being blamed when they do not.

Right across the way from Mrs. Standfast is Mrs. Easy, a pretty little creature, with not a tithe of her moral worth,—a merry, pleasure-loving woman, of no particular force of principle, whose great object in life is to avoid its disagreeables and to secure its pleasures.

Little Mrs. Easy is adored by her husband, her children, her servants, merely because it is her nature to say pleasant things to every one. It is a mere tact of pleasing which she uses without knowing it. While Mrs. Standfast, surveying her well-set dining-table, runs her keen eye over everything, and at last brings up with, "Jane, look at that black spot on the salt-spoon! I am astonished at your carelessness!"—Mrs. Easy would say, "Why, Jane, where *did* you learn to set a table so nicely? All looking beautifully, except—ah! let's see—just give a rub to this salt-spoon;—now all is quite perfect." Mrs. Standfast's servants and children hear only of their failures; these are always before them and her. Mrs. Easy's servants hear of their successes. She praises their good points; tells them they are doing well in this, that, and the other particular; and finally exhorts them, on the strength of having done so many things well, to improve in what is yet lacking. Mrs. Easy's husband feels that he is always a hero in her eyes, and her children feel that they are dear good children, notwithstanding Mrs. Easy sometimes has her little tiffs of displeasure, and scolds roundly when something falls out as it should not.

The two families show how much more may be done by a very ordinary woman, through the mere instinct of praising and pleasing, than by the greatest worth, piety, and principle, seeking to lift human nature by a lever that never was meant to lift it by.

The faults and mistakes of us poor human beings are as often perpetuated by despair as by any other one thing. Have we not all been burdened by a consciousness of faults that we were slow to correct because we felt discouraged? Have we not been sensible of a real help sometimes from the presence of a friend who thought well of us, believed in us, set our virtues in the best light, and put our faults in the background?

Let us depend upon it, that the flesh and blood that are in us—the needs, the wants, the despondencies—

are in each of our fellows, in every awkward servant and careless child.

Finally, let us all resolve,—

First, to attain to the grace of SILENCE.

Second, to deem all FAULT-FINDING that does no good, a SIN; and to resolve, when we are happy ourselves, not to poison the atmosphere for our neighbours by calling on them to remark every painful and disagreeable feature of their daily life.

Third, to practise the grace and virtue of PRAISE. We have all been taught that it is our duty to praise God, but few of us have reflected on our duty to praise men; and yet, for the same reason that we should praise the divine goodness, it is our duty to praise human excellence.

We should praise our friends,—our near and dear ones; we should look on and think of their virtues till their faults fade away; and when we love most, and see most to love, then only is the wise time wisely to speak of what should still be altered.

Parents should look out for occasions to commend their children, as carefully as they seek to reprove their faults; and employers should praise the good their servants do as strictly as they blame the evil.

Whoever undertakes to use this weapon will find that praise goes farther in many cases than blame. Watch till a blundering servant does something well, and then praise him for it, and you will see a new fire lighted in the eye, and often you will find that in that one respect at least you have secured excellence thenceforward.

When you blame, which should be seldom, let it be alone with the person, quietly, considerately, and with all the tact you are possessed of. The fashion of reproving children and servants in the presence of others cannot be too much deprecated. Pride, stubbornness, and self-will are aroused by this, while a more private reproof might be received with thankfulness.

As a general rule, I would say, treat children in these respects just as you would grown people; they are grown people in miniature, and need as careful consideration of their feelings as any of us.

Lastly, let us all make a bead-roll, a holy rosary, of all that is good and agreeable in our position, our surroundings, our daily lot, of all that is good and agreeable in our friends, our children, our servants, and charge ourselves to repeat it daily, till the habit of our minds be to praise and to commend; and so doing, we shall catch and kill one *Little Fox* who hath destroyed many tender grapes.

II.

IRRITABILITY.

IT was that Christmas-day that did it; I'm quite convinced of that; and the way it was is what I am going to tell you.

You see, among the various family customs of us Crowfields, the observance of all sorts of *fêtes* and festivals has always been a matter of prime regard; and among all the festivals of the round, ripe year, none is so joyous and honoured among us as Christmas.

Let no one upon this prick up the ears of Archæology, and tell us that by the latest calculations of chronologists our ivy-grown and holly-mantled Christmas is all a hum,—that it has been demonstrated, by all sorts of signs and tables, that the august event it celebrates did not take place on the 25th of December. Supposing it be so, what have we to do with that? If so awful, so joyous an event ever took place on our earth, it is surely worth commemoration. It is the *event* we celebrate, not the *time*. And if all Christians for eighteen hundred years, while warring and wrangling on a thousand other points, have agreed to give this one 25th of December to peace and good-will, who is he that shall gainsay them, and, for an historic scruple, turn his back on the friendly greetings of Christendom? Such a man is capable of rewriting

Milton's Christmas Hymn in the style of Sternhold and Hopkins.

In our house, however, Christmas has always been a high day, a day whose expectation has held waking all the little eyes in our bird's nest, when as yet there were only little ones there, each sleeping with one eye open, hoping to be the happy first to wish the merry Christmas and grasp the wonderful stocking.

This year, our whole family train of married girls and boys, with the various toddling tribes thereto belonging, held high festival around a wonderful Christmas-tree, the getting-up and adorning of which had kept my wife and Jennie and myself busy for a week beforehand. If the little folks think these trees grow up in a night, without labour, they know as little about them as they do about most of the other blessings which rain down on their little thoughtless heads. Such scrambling and clambering and fussing and tying and untying, such alterations and rearrangements, such agilities in getting up and down and everywhere, to tie on tapers and gold balls and glittering things innumerable,—to hang airy dolls in graceful positions,—to make branches bear stiffly up under loads of pretty things which threaten to make the tapers turn bottom upward! Part and parcel of all this was I, Christopher, most reckless of rheumatism, most careless of dignity, the round, bald top of my head to be seen emerging everywhere from the thick boughs of the spruce, now devising an airy settlement for some gossamer-robed doll, now adjusting far back on a stiff branch Tom's new little skates, now balancing bags of sugar-plums and candy, and now combating desperately with some contumacious taper that would turn slantwise or crosswise, or anywise but upward as a Christian taper should, — regardless of Mrs. Crowfield's gentle admonitions and suggestions, sitting up to most dissipated hours, springing out of bed suddenly, to change some arrangement in the middle of the night, and up at dawn, long before the lazy sun, to execute still other arrangements. If that Christmas-tree had been a fort to be taken, or a campaign to be planned, I could not have spent more time and strength on it. My zeal so far outran even that of sprightly Miss Jennie, that she could account for it only by saucily suggesting that papa must be fast getting into second childhood.

But didn't we have a splendid lighting-up? Didn't I and my youngest grandson, little Tom, head the procession magnificent in paper soldier caps, blowing tin trumpets and beating drums, as we marched round the twinkling glories of our Christmas-tree, all glittering with red and blue and green tapers, and with a splendid angel on top with great gold wings, the cutting-out and adjusting of which had held my eyes waking for nights before? I had had oceans of trouble with that angel, owing to an unlucky sprain in his left wing, which had required constant surgical attention through the week, and which I feared might fall loose again at the important and blissful moment of exhibition: but no, the Fates were in our favour; the angel behaved beautifully, and kept his wings as crisp as possible, and the tapers all burned splendidly, and the little folks were as crazy with delight as my most ardent hopes could have desired; and then we romped and played and frolicked as long as little eyes could keep open, and long after; and so passed away our Christmas.

I had forgotten to speak of the Christmas-dinner, that solid feast of fat things on which we also luxuriated. Mrs. Crowfield outdid all household traditions in that feast: the turkey and the chickens, the jellies and the sauces, the pies and the pudding, behold, are they not written in the tablets of Memory which remain to this day?

The holidays passed away hilariously, and at New-Year's-Day I, according to time-honoured custom, went forth to make my calls and see my fair friends, while my wife and daughters stayed at home to dispense the hospitalities of the day to their gentlemen friends. All was merry, cheerful, and it was agreed on all hands that a more joyous holiday season had never flown over us.

But, somehow, the week after, I began to be sensible of a running-down in the wheels. I had an article to write for the *Atlantic*, but felt mopish and could not write. My dinner had not its usual relish, and I had an indefinite sense everywhere of something going wrong. My coal-bill came in, and I felt sure we were being extravagant, and that our John Furnace wasted the coal. My grandsons and granddaughters came to see us, and I discovered that they had high-pitched voices, and burst in without wiping their shoes, and it suddenly occurred powerfully to my mind that they were not being well brought up,—evidently, they were growing up rude and noisy. I discovered several tumblers and plates with the edges chipped, and made bitter reflections on the carelessness of Irish servants; our crockery was going to destruction, along with the rest. Then, on opening one of my paper-drawers, I found that Jennie's one drawer of worsted had overflowed into two or three; Jennie was growing careless; besides, worsted is dear, and girls knit away small fortunes without knowing it, on little duds that do nobody any good. Moreover, Maggie had three times put my slippers into the hall-closet, instead of leaving them where I wanted, under my study-table. Mrs. Crowfield ought to look after things more; every servant, from end to end of the house, was getting out of the traces; it was strange she did not see it.

All this I vented from time to time, in short, crusty sayings and doings, as freely as if I hadn't just written an article on "Little Foxes" in the last *Atlantic*, till at length my eyes were opened on my own state and condition.

It was evening, and I had just laid up the fire in the most approved style of architecture, and projecting my feet into my slippers, sat spitefully cutting the leaves of a caustic review.

Mrs. Crowfield took the tongs and altered the disposition of a stick.

"My dear," I said, "I do wish you'd let the fire alone,—you always put it out."

"I was merely admitting a little air between the sticks," said my wife.

"You always make matters worse when you touch the fire."

As if in contradiction, a bright tongue of flame darted up between the sticks, and the fire began chattering and snapping defiance at me. Now, if there's anything which would provoke a saint, it is to be jeered and snapped at in that way by a man's own fire. It 's an unbearable impertinence. I threw out my leg impatiently, and hit Rover, who yelped a yelp that finished the upset of my nerves. I gave him a hearty kick, that he might have something to yelp for, and in the movement upset Jennie's embroidery-basket.

"Oh, papa!"

"Confound your baskets and balls! they are everywhere, so that a man can't move; useless, wasteful things, too."

"Wasteful?" said Jennie, colouring indignantly; for if there's anything Jennie piques herself upon, it's economy.

"Yes, wasteful,—wasting time and money both. Here are hundreds of shivering poor to be clothed, and Christian females sit and do nothing but crochet worsted into useless knick-nacks. If they would be working for the poor there would be some sense in it; but it's all just alike, no real Christianity in the world,—nothing but organized selfishness and self-indulgence."

"My dear," said Mrs. Crowfield, "you are not well tonight. Things are not quite so desperate as they appear. You haven't got over Christmas-week."

"I am well. Never was better. But I can see, I hope, what's before my eyes; and the fact is, Mrs. Crowfield, things must not go on as they are going. There must be more care, more attention to details. There's Maggie,—that girl never does what she is told. You are too slack with her, Ma'am. She will light the fire with the last paper, and she won't put my slippers in the right place; and I can't have my study made the general catch-all and menagerie for Rover and Jennie, and her baskets and balls, and for all the family litter."

Just at this moment I overheard a sort of aside from Jennie, who was swelling with repressed indignation at my attack on her worsted. She sat with her back to me, knitting energetically, and said, in a low, but very decisive tone, as she twitched her yarn,—

"Now if *I* should talk in that way, people would call me *cross*,—and that's the whole of it."

I pretended to be looking into the fire in an absent-minded state; but Jennie's words had started a new idea. Was *that* it? Was it, then, a fact, that the house, the servants, Jennie and her worsteds, Rover and Mrs. Crowfield, were all going on pretty much as usual, and that the only difficulty was that I was *cross?* How many times had I encouraged Rover to lie just where he was lying when I kicked him! How many times, in better moods, had I complimented Jennie on her neat little fancy-works, and declared that I liked the social companionship of ladies' work-baskets among my papers!

Yes, it was clear. After all, things were much as they had been; only I was cross.

Cross. I put it to myself in that simple, old-fashioned word, instead of saying that I was out of spirits, or nervous, or using any of the other smooth phrases with which we good Christians cover up our little sins of temper. "Here you are, Christopher," said I to myself, "a literary man, with a somewhat delicate nervous organization and a sensitive stomach, and you have been eating like a sailor or a ploughman; you have been gallivanting and merry-making and playing the boy for two weeks; up at all sorts of irregular hours, and into all sorts of boyish performances; and the consequence is, that, like a thoughtless young scapegrace, you have used up in ten days the capital of nervous energy that was meant to last you ten weeks. You can't eat your cake and have it too, Christopher. When the nervous-fluid source of cheerfulness, giver of pleasant sensations and pleasant views, is all spent, you can't feel cheerful; things cannot look as they did when you were full of life and vigour. When the tide is out, there is nothing but unsightly, ill-smelling tide-mud, and you can't help it; but you can keep your senses,—you can know what is the matter with you,—you can keep from visiting your overdose of Christmas mince-pies and candies and jocularities on the heads of Mrs. Crowfield, Rover, and Jennie, whether in the form of virulent morality, pungent criticisms, or a free kick, such as you just gave the poor brute."

"Come here, Rover, poor dog!" said I, extending my

hand to Rover, who cowered at the farther corner of the room, eyeing me wistfully,—"come here, you poor doggie, and make up with your master. There, there! Was his master cross? Well, he knows it. We must forgive and forget, old boy, mustn't we?" And Rover nearly broke his own back and tore me to pieces with his tumultuous tail-waggings.

"As for you, puss," I said to Jennie, "I am much obliged to you for your free suggestion. You must take my cynical moralities for what they are worth, and put your little traps into as many of my drawers as you like."

In short, I made it up handsomely all around,—even apologizing to Mrs. Crowfield, who, by-the-by, has summered and wintered me so many years, and knows all my airs and cuts and crinkles so well, that she took my irritable, unreasonable spirit as tranquilly as if I had been a baby cutting a new tooth.

"Of course, Chris, I knew what the matter was; don't disturb yourself," she said, as I began my apology; "we understand each other. But there is one thing I have to say; and that is, that your article ought to be ready."

"Ah, well, then," said I, "like other great writers, I shall make capital of my own sins, and treat of the second little family fox; and his name is—

IRRITABILITY.

IRRITABILITY is, more than most unlovely states, a sin of the flesh. It is not, like envy, malice, spite, revenge, a vice which we may suppose to belong equally to an embodied or a disembodied spirit: in fact, it comes nearer to being physical depravity than anything I know of. There are some bodily states, some conditions of the nerves, such that we could not conceive of even an angelic spirit, confined in a body thus disordered, as being able to do any more than simply endure. It is a state of nervous torture; and the attacks which the wretched victim makes on others are as much a result of disease as the snapping and biting of a patient convulsed with hydrophobia.

Then, again, there are other people who go through life loving and beloved, desired in every circle, held up in the church as examples of the power of religion, who, after all, deserve no credit for these things. Their spirits are lodged in an animal nature so tranquil, so cheerful, all the sensations which come to them are so fresh and vigorous and pleasant, that they cannot help viewing the world charitably, and seeing everything through a glorified medium. The ill-temper of others does not provoke them; perplexing business never sets their nerves to vibrating; and all their lives long they walk in the serene sunshine of perfect animal health.

Look at Rover there. He is never nervous, never cross, never snaps or snarls, and is ready, the moment after the grossest affront, to wag the tail of forgiveness, —all because kind Nature has put his dog's body together so that it always works harmoniously. If every person in the world were gifted with a stomach and nerves like his, it would be a far better and happier world, no doubt. The man said a good thing who made the remark that the foundation of all intellectual and moral worth must be laid in a good healthy animal.

Now I think it is undeniable that the peace and happiness of the home-circle are very generally much invaded by the recurrence in its members of these states of bodily irritability. Every person, if he thinks the matter over, will see that his condition in life, the character of his friends, his estimate of their virtues and failings, his hopes and expectations, are all very much modified by these things. Cannot we all remember going to bed as very ill-used, persecuted individuals, all whose friends were unreasonable, whose life was full of trials and crosses, and waking up on a bright bird-singing morning to find all these illusions gone with the fogs of the night? Our friends are nice people, after all; the little things that annoyed us look ridiculous by bright sunshine; and we are fortunate individuals.

The philosophy of life, then, as far as this matter is concerned, must consist of two things: first, to keep ourselves out of irritable bodily states; and, second, to understand and control these states, when we cannot ward them off.

Of course, the first of these is the most important; and yet, of all things, it seems to be least looked into and understood. We find abundant rules for the government of the tongue and temper; it is a slough into which, John Bunyan hath it, cart-loads of wholesome instructions have been thrown; but how to get and keep that healthy state of brain, stomach, and nerves which takes away the temptation to ill-temper and anger is a subject which moral and religious teachers seem scarcely to touch upon.

Now, without running into technical, physiological language, it is evident, as regards us human beings, that there is a power by which we live and move and have our being,—by which the brain thinks and wills, the stomach digests, the blood circulates, and all the different provinces of the little man-kingdom do their work. This something—call it nervous fluid, nervous power, vital energy, life-force, or anything else that you will—is a perfectly understood, if not a definable thing. It is plain, too, that people possess this force in very different degrees: some generating it as a high-pressure engine does steam, and using it constantly, with an apparently inexhaustible flow; and others who have little, and spend it quickly. We have a common saying, that this or that person is soon used up. Now most nervous, irritable states of temper are the mere physical result of a used-up condition. The person has overspent his nervous energy,—like a man who should eat up on Monday the whole food which was to keep him for a week, and go growling and faint through the other days; or the quantity of nervous force which was wanted to carry on the whole system in all its parts is seized on by some one monopolizing portion, and used up to the loss and detriment of the rest. Thus, with men of letters, an exorbitant brain expends on its own workings what belongs to the other offices of the body; the stomach has nothing to carry on digestion; the secretions are badly made; and the imperfectly assimilated nourishment that is conveyed to every little nerve and tissue, carries with it an acrid, irritating quality, producing general restlessness and discomfort. So men and women go struggling on through their threescore and ten years, scarcely one in a thousand knowing through life that perfect balance of parts, that appropriate harmony of energies, that make a healthy, kindly animal condition, predisposing to cheerfulness and good-will.

We Americans are, to begin with, a nervous, excitable people. Multitudes of children, probably the great majority in the upper walks of life, are born into the world with weaknesses of the nervous organization, or of the brain or stomach, which make them incapable of any strong excitement or prolonged exertion without some lesion or derangement; so that they are continually being checked, laid up, and invalided in the midst of their drugs. Life here in America is so fervid, so fast, our climate is so stimulating, with its clear, bright skies, its rapid and sudden changes of temperature, that the tendencies to nervous disease are constantly aggravated.

Under these circumstances, unless men and women make a conscience, a religion, of saving and sparing something of themselves expressly for home-life and home-consumption, it must follow that home will often be merely a sort of refuge for us to creep into when we are used up and irritable.

Papa is up and off, after a hasty breakfast, and drives all day in his business, putting into it all there is in him, letting it drink up brain and nerve and body and soul, and coming home jaded and exhausted, so that he cannot bear the cry of the baby, and the frolics and pattering of the nursery seem horrid and needless confusion. The little ones say, in their plain vernacular, "Papa is cross."

Mamma goes out to a party that keeps her up till one or two in the morning, breathes bad air, eats indigestible food, and the next day is so nervous that every straw and thread in her domestic path is insufferable.

Papas that pursue business thus, day after day, and mammas that go into company, as it is called, night after night, what is there left in or of them to make an agreeable fireside with, to brighten their home and inspire their children?

True, the man says he cannot help himself,—business requires it. But what is the need of rolling up money at the rate at which he is seeking to do it? Why not have less, and take some time to enjoy his home, and cheer up his wife, and form the minds of his children? Why spend himself down to the last drop on the world, and give to the dearest friends he has only the bitter dregs?

Much of the preaching which the pulpit and the Church have levelled at fashionable amusements has failed of any effect at all, because wrongly put. A cannonade has been opened upon dancing, for example, and all for reasons that will not, in the least, bear looking into. It is vain to talk of dancing as a sin because practised in a dying world where souls are passing into eternity. If dancing is a sin for this reason, so is playing marbles, or frolicking with one's children, or enjoying a good dinner, or doing fifty other things which nobody ever dreamed of objecting to.

If the preacher were to say that anything is a sin which uses up the strength we need for daily duties, and leaves us fagged out and irritable at just those times and in just those places when and where we need most to be healthy, cheerful, and self-possessed, he would say a thing that none of his hearers would dispute. If he should add, that dancing-parties, beginning at ten o'clock at night and ending at four o'clock in the morning, do use up the strength, weaken the nerves, and leave a person wholly unfit for any home duty, he would also be saying what very few people would deny; and then his case would be made out. If he should say that it is wrong to breathe bad air and fill the stomach with unwholesome dainties, so as to make one restless, ill-natured, and irritable for days after, he would also say what few would deny, and his preaching might have some hope of success.

The true manner of judging of the worth of amusements is to try them by their effects on the nerves and spirits the day after. True amusement ought to be, as the word indicates, recreation,—something that refreshes, turns us out anew, rests the body and mind by change, and gives cheerfulness and alacrity to our return to duty.

The true objection to all stimulants, alcoholic and narcotic, consists simply in this,—that they are a form of overdraft on the nervous energy, which helps us to use up in one hour the strength of whole days.

A man uses up all the fair, legal interest of nervous power by too much business, too much care, or too much amusement. He has now a demand to meet. He has a complicate account to make up, an essay or a sermon to write, and he primes himself by a cup of coffee, a cigar, a glass of spirits. This is exactly the procedure of a man who, having used the interest of his money, begins to dip into the principal. The strength a man gets in this way is just so much taken out of his life-blood; it is borrowing of a merciless creditor, who will exact, in time, the pound of flesh nearest his heart.

Much of the irritability which spoils home happiness is the letting down from the over-excitement of stimulus. Some will drink coffee, when they own every day that it makes them nervous; some will drug themselves with tobacco, and some with alcohol, and, for a few hours of extra brightness, give themselves and their friends many hours when amiability or agreeableness is quite out of the question. There are people calling themselves Christians who live in miserable thraldom, for ever in debt to Nature, for ever overdrawing on their just resources, and using up their patrimony, because they have not the moral courage to break away from a miserable appetite.

The same may be said of numberless indulgences of the palate, which tax the stomach beyond its power, and bring on all the horrors of indigestion. It is almost impossible for a confirmed dyspeptic to act like a good Christian; but a good Christian ought not to become a confirmed dyspeptic. Reasonable self-control, abstaining from all unseasonable indulgence, may prevent or put an end to dyspepsia, and many suffer and make their friends suffer only because they will persist in eating what they know is hurtful to them.

But it is not merely in worldly business, or fashionable amusements, or the gratification of appetite, that people are tempted to overdraw and use up in advance their life-force: it is done in ways more insidious, because connected with our moral and religious faculties. There are religious exaltations beyond the regular pulse and beatings of ordinary nature, that quite as surely gravitate downward into the mire of irritability. The ascent to the third heaven lets even the Apostle down to a thorn in the flesh, the messenger of Satan to buffet him.

It is the temptation to natures in which the moral faculties predominate to overdo in the outward expression and activities of religion till they are used up and irritable, and have no strength left to set a good example in domestic life.

The Reverend Mr. X. in the pulpit to-day appears with the face of an angel; he soars away into those regions of exalted devotion where his people can but faintly gaze after him; he tells them of the victory that overcometh the world, of an unmoved faith that fears no evil, of a serenity of love that no outward event can ruffle; and all look after him and wonder, and wish they could so soar.

Alas! the exaltation which inspires these sublime conceptions, these celestial ecstasies, is a double and treble draft on Nature,—and poor Mrs. X. knows when she hears him preaching, that days of miserable reaction are before her. He has been a fortnight driving before a gale of strong excitement, doing all the time twice or thrice as much as in his ordinary state he could, and sustaining himself by the stimulus of strong coffee. He has preached or exhorted every night, and conversed with religious inquirers every day, seeming to himself to become stronger and stronger, because every day more and more excitable and excited. To his hearers, with his flushed sunken cheek and his glittering eye, he looks like some spiritual being just trembling on his flight for upper worlds; but to poor Mrs. X., whose husband he is, things wear a very different aspect. Her woman and mother instincts tell her that he is drawing on his life-capital with both hands, and that the hours of a terrible settlement must come, and the days of darkness will be many. He who spoke so beautifully of the peace of a soul made perfect will not be able to bear the cry of his baby or the pattering feet of any of the poor little Xs., who must be sent

> "Anywhere, anywhere,
> Out of his sight;"

he who discoursed so devoutly of perfect trust in God will be nervous about the butcher's bill, sure of going to ruin because both ends of the salary don't meet; and he who could so admiringly tell of the silence of Jesus under prvoocation will but too often speak unadvisedly with his lips. Poor Mr. X. will be morally insane for days or weeks, and absolutely incapable of preaching Christ in the way that is the most effective, by setting him forth in his own daily example.

What then? must we not do the work of the Lord?

Yes, certainly; but the first work of the Lord, that for which provision is to be made in the first place, is to set a good example as a Christian man. Better labour for years steadily, diligently, doing every day only what the night's rest can repair, avoiding those cheating stimulants that overtax Nature, and illustrating the sayings of the pulpit by the daily life in the family, than to pass life in exaltations and depressions.

The same principles apply to hearers as to preachers. Religious services must be judged of like amusements, by their effect on the life. If an overdose of prayers, hymns, and sermons leaves us tired, nervous, and cross, it is only not quite as bad as an overdose of fashionable folly.

It could be wished that in every neighbourhood there might be one or two calm, sweet, daily services which should morning and evening unite for a few solemn moments the hearts of all as in one family, and feed with a constant, unnoticed, daily supply, the lamp of faith and love. Such are some of the daily prayer-meetings which for eight or ten years past have held their even tenor in some of our New England cities, and such the morning and evening services which we are glad to see obtaining in the Episcopal churches. Everything which brings religion into habitual contact with life, and makes it part of a healthy, cheerful average living, we hail as a sign of a better day. Nothing is so good for health as daily devotion. It is the best soother of the nerves, the best antidote to care; and we trust ere long that all Christian people will be of one mind in this, and that neighbourhoods will be families gathering daily around one altar, praying not for themselves merely, but for each other.

The conclusion of the whole matter is this: Set apart some provision to make merry with *at home*, and guard that reserve as religiously as the priests guarded the shew-bread in the temple. However great you are, however good, however wide the general interests that you may control, you gain nothing by neglecting home-duties. You must leave enough of yourself to be able to bear and forbear, give and forgive, and be a source of life and cheerfulness around the hearthstone. The great sign given by the Prophets of the coming of the Millennium is,—what do you suppose?—"He shall turn the heart of the fathers to the children, and the heart of the children to their fathers, lest I come and smite the earth with a curse."

Thus much on avoiding unhealthy, irritable states.

But it still remains that a large number of people will be subject to them unavoidably; for these reasons—

First. The use of tobacco, alcohol, and other kindred stimulants, for so many generations, has vitiated the brain and nervous system, so that it is not what it was in former times. Michelet treats of this subject quite at large in some of his late works; and we have to face the fact of a generation born with an impaired nervous organization, who will need constant care and wisdom to avoid unhealthy, morbid irritation.

There is a temperament called the HYPOCHONDRIAC, to which many persons, some of them the brightest, the most interesting, the most gifted, are born heirs,—a want of balance of the nervous powers, which tends constantly to periods of high excitement and of consequent depression,—an unfortunate inheritance for the possessor, though accompanied often with the greatest talents. Sometimes, too, it is the unfortunate lot of those who have not talents, who bear its burdens and its anguish without its rewards.

People of this temperament are subject to fits of gloom and despondency, of nervous irritability and suffering, which darken the aspect of the whole world to them, which present lying reports of their friends, of themselves, of the circumstances of their life, and of all with which they have to do.

Now the highest philosophy for persons thus afflicted is to understand themselves and their tendencies, to know that these fits of gloom and depression are just as much a form of disease as a fever or a toothache,—to know that it is the peculiarity of the disease to fill the mind with wretched illusions, to make them seem miserable and unlovely to themselves, to make their nearest friends seem unjust and unkind, to make all events appear to be going wrong and tending to destruction and ruin.

The evils and burdens of such a temperament are half

removed when a man once knows that he has it, and recognizes it for a disease,—when he does not trust himself to speak and act in those bitter hours as if there were any truth in what he thinks and feels and sees. He who has not attained to this wisdom overwhelms his friends and his family with the waters of bitterness; he stings with unjust accusations, and makes his fireside dreadful with fancies which are real to him, but false as the ravings of fever.

A sensible person, thus diseased, who has found out what ails him, will shut his mouth resolutely, not to give utterauce to the dark thoughts that infest his soul.

A lady of great brilliancy and wit, who was subject to these periods, once said to me, "My dear sir, there are times when I know I am possessed of the Devil, and then I never let myself speak." And so this wise woman carried her burden about with her in a determined, cheerful reticence, leaving always the impression of a cheery, kindly temper, when, if she had spoken out a tithe of what she thought and felt in her morbid hours, she would have driven all her friends from her, and made others as miserable as she was herself. She was a sunbeam, a life-giving presence in every family, by the power of self-knowledge and self-control.

Such victories as this are the victories of real saints.

But if the victim of these glooms is once tempted to lift their heavy load by the use of *any stimulus whatever*, he or she is a lost man or woman. It is from this sad class more than any other that the vast army of drunkards and opium-eaters is recruited. The hypochondriacs belong to the class so well described by that brilliant specimen of them, Dr. Johnson,—those who can practise ABSTINENCE, but not TEMPERANCE. They cannot, they will not be moderate. Whatever stimulant they take for relief will create an uncontrollable appetite—a burning passion. The temperament itself lies in the direction of insanity. It needs the most healthful, careful, even regime and management to keep it within the bounds of soundness; but the introduction of stimulants deepens its gloom almost to madness.

All parents, in the education of their children, should look out for and understand the signs of this temperament. It appears in early childhood; and a child inclined to fits of depression should be marked as a subject of the most thoughtful, painstaking physical and moral training. All over-excitement and stimulus should be carefully avoided, whether in the way of study, amusement, or diet. Judicious education may do much to mitigate the unavoidable pains and penalties of this most undesirable inheritance.

The second class of persons who need wisdom in the control of their moods is that large class whose unfortunate circumstances make it impossible for them to avoid constantly overdoing and overdrawing upon their nervous energies, and who, therefore, are always exhausted and worn out. Poor souls, who labour daily under a burden too heavy for them, and whose fretfulness and impatience are looked upon with sorrow, not anger, by pitying angels. Poor mothers, with families of little children clinging round them, and a baby that never lets them sleep; hard-working men, whose utmost toil, day and night, scarcely keeps the wolf from the door; and all the hard-labouring, heavy-laden, on whom the burdens of life press far beyond their strength.

There are but two things we know of for these,—two only remedies for the irritation that comes of these exhaustions: the habit of silence towards men, and of speech towards God. The heart must utter itself or burst; but let it learn to commune constantly and intimately with One always present and always sympathizing. This is the great, the only safeguard against fretfulness and complaint. Thus and thus only can peace spring out of confusion, and the breaking chords of an overtaxed nature be strung anew to a celestial harmony.

III.

REPRESSION.

Being the true copy of a paper read in my library to my Wife and Jennie.

I AM going now to write on another cause of family unhappiness, more subtile than either of those before enumerated.

In the General Confession of the Church, we poor mortals all unite in saying two things: "We have left undone those things which we ought to have done, and we have done those things which we ought not to have done." These two heads exhaust the subject of human frailty.

It is the things left undone which we ought to have done, the things left unsaid which we ought to have said, that constitute the subject I am now to treat of.

I remember my school-day speculations over an old "Chemistry" I used to study as a text-book, which informed me that a substance called Caloric exists in all bodies. In some it exists in a latent state: it is there, but it affects neither the senses nor the thermometer. Certain causes develop it when it raises the mercury and warms the hands. I remember the awe and wonder with which, even then, I reflected on the vast amount of blind, deaf, and dumb comforts which nature had thus stowed away. How mysterious it seemed to me that poor families every winter should be shivering, freezing, and catching cold, when Nature had all this latent caloric locked up in her store-closet,—when it was all around them, in everything they touched and handled.

In the spiritual world there is an exact analogy to this. There is a great life-giving, warming power called Love, which exists in human hearts dumb and unseen, but which has no real life, no warming power, till set free by expression.

Did you ever, in a raw, chilly day, just before a snow-storm, sit at work in a room that was judiciously warmed by an exact thermometer? You do not freeze, but you shiver; your fingers do not become numb with cold, but you have all the while an uneasy craving for more positive warmth. You look at the empty grate, walk mechanically towards it, and, suddenly awaking, shiver to see that there is nothing there. You long for a shawl or cloak; you draw yourself within yourself; you consult the thermometer, and are vexed to find that there is nothing there to be complained of,—it is standing most provokingly at the exact temperature that all the good books and good doctors pronounce to be the proper thing—the golden mean of health; and yet perversely you shiver, and feel as if the face of an open fire would be to you as the smile of an angel.

Such a lifelong chill, such an habitual shiver is the

lot of many natures, which are not warm, when all ordinary rules tell them they ought to be warm,— whose life is cold and barren and meagre,—which never see the blaze of an open fire.

I will illustrate my meaning by a page out of my own experience.

I was twenty-one when I stood as groomsman for my youngest and favourite sister Emily. I remember her now as she stood at the altar,—a pale, sweet, flowery face, in a half-shimmer between smiles and tears, looking out of vapoury clouds of gauze and curls, and all the vanishing mysteries of a bridal morning.

Everybody thought the marriage such a fortunate one!—for her husband was handsome and manly, a man of worth, of principle good as gold and solid as adamant, —and Emmy had always been such a flossy little kitten of a pet, so full of all sorts of impulses, so sensitive and nervous, we thought her kind, strong, composed, stately husband made just on purpose for her. "It was quite a providence," sighed all the elderly ladies, who sniffed tenderly, and wiped their eyes, according to approved custom, during the marriage ceremony.

I remember now the bustle of the day,—the confused whirl of white gloves, kisses, bridemaids, and bride-cakes, the losing of trunk keys, and breaking of lacings, the tears of mamma—God bless her!—and the jokes of irreverent Christopher, who could, for the life of him, see nothing so very dismal in the whole phantasmagoria, and only wished he were as well off himself.

And so Emmy was wheeled away from us on the

bridal tour, when her letters came back to us almost every day, just like herself, merry, frisky little bits of scratches,—as full of little nonsense beads as a glass of champagne, and all ending with telling us how perfect he was, and how good, and how well he took care of her, and how happy, etc., etc.

Then came letters from her new home. His house was not yet built; but while it was building they were to live with his mother, who was "such a good woman," and his sisters, who were also "such nice women."

But somehow, after this, a change came over Emmy's letters. They grew shorter; they seemed measured in their words; and in place of sparkling nonsense and bubbling outbursts of glee, came anxiously worded praises of her situation and surroundings, evidently written for the sake of arguing herself into the belief that she was extremely happy.

John, of course, was not as much with her now: he had his business to attend to, which took him away all day, and at night he was very tired. Still he was very good and thoughtful of her, and how thankful she ought to be! And his mother was very good indeed, and did all for her that she could reasonably expect,—of course she could not be like her own mamma; and Mary and Jane were very kind,—"in their way," she wrote, but scratched it out, and wrote over it "very kind indeed." They were the best people in the world,—a great deal better than she was; and she should try to learn a great deal from them.

"Poor little Em!" I said to myself, "I am afraid these very nice people are slowly freezing and starving her." And so, as I was going up into the mountains for a summer tour, I thought I would accept some of John's many invitations, and stop a day or two with them on my way, and see how matters stood. John had been known among us in college as a taciturn fellow, but good as gold. I had gained his friendship by a regular siege, carrying parallel after parallel, till, when I came into the fort at last, I found the treasures worth taking.

I had little difficulty in finding Squire Evans's house, It was *the* house of the village,—a true, model, New England house,—a square, roomy, old-fashioned mansion, which stood on a hill-side under a group of great, breezy old elms, whose wide, wind-swung arms arched over it like a leafy firmament. Under this bower the substantial white house, with all its window-blinds closed, with its neat white fences all tight and trim, stood in its faultless green turfy yard, a perfect Pharisee among houses. It looked like a house all finished, done, completed, labelled, and set on a shelf for preservation; but, as is usual with this kind of edifice in our dear New England, it had not the slightest appearance of being lived in, not a door or window open, not a wink or blink of life: the only suspicion of human habitation was the thin, pale-blue smoke from the kitchen chimney.

And now for the people in the house.

In making a New England visit in winter, was it ever your fortune to be put to sleep in the glacial spare chamber, that had been kept from time immemorial as a refrigerator for guests,—that room which no ray of daily sunshine and daily living ever warms, whose blinds are closed the whole year round, whose fireplace knows only the complimentary blaze which is kindled a few moments before bed-time in an atmosphere where you can see your breath? Do you remember the process of getting warm in a bed of most faultless material, with linen sheets and pillow-cases, slippery and cold as ice? You did get warm at last, but you warmed your bed by giving out all the heat of your own body.

Such are some families where you visit. They are of the very best quality, like your sheets, but so cold that it takes all the vitality you have to get them warmed up to the talking-point. You think, the first hour after your arrival, that they must have heard some report to your disadvantage, or that you misunderstood your letter of invitation, or that you came on the wrong day; but no, you find in due course that you *were* invited, you *were* expected, and they are doing for you the best they can, and treating you as they suppose a guest ought to be treated.

If you are a warm-hearted, jovial fellow, and go on feeling your way discreetly, you gradually thaw quite a little place round yourself in the domestic circle, till, by the time you are ready to leave, you really begin to think it is agreeable to stay, and resolve that you will come again. They are nice people; they like you; at last you have got to feeling at home with them.

Three months after, you go to see them again, when lo! there you are, back again just where you were at first. The little spot which you had thawed out is frozen over again, and again you spend all your visit in thawing it and getting your hosts limbered and in a state for comfortable converse.

The first evening that I spent in the wide, roomy front parlour, with Judge Evans, his wife, and daughters, fully accounted for the change in Emmy's letters. Rooms, I verily believe, get saturated with the aroma of their spiritual atmosphere; and there are some so stately, so correct, that they would paralyze even the friskiest kitten, or the most impudent Scotch terrier. At a glance you perceive, on entering, that nothing but correct deportment, an erect posture, and strictly didactic conversation is possible there.

The family, in fact, were all eminently didactic,—bent on improvement, laboriously useful. Not a good work or charitable enterprise could put forth its head in the neighbourhood, of which they were not the support and life. Judge Evans was the stay and staff of the village and township of ——; he bore up the pillars thereof. Mrs. Evans was known in the gates for all the properties and deeds of the virtuous woman, as set forth by Solomon; the heart of her husband did safely trust in her. But when I saw them that evening, sitting, in erect propriety, in their respective corners on each side of the great, stately fireplace, with its tall, glistening brass andirons, its mantel adorned at either end with plated candlesticks, with the snuffer-tray in the middle,—she so collectedly measuring her words, talking in all those well-worn grooves of correct conversation which are designed, as the phrase goes, to "entertain strangers," and the Misses Evans, in the best of grammar and rhetoric, and in most proper time and way possible, showing themselves for what they were, most high-principled, well-informed, intelligent women,—I set myself to speculate on the cause of the extraordinary sensation of stiffness and restraint which pervaded me, as if I had been dipped in some petrifying spring, and was beginning to feel myself slightly crusting over on the exterior.

This kind of conversation is such as admits quite easily of one's carrying on another course of thought within; and so, as I found myself like a machine, striking in now and then in good time and tune, I looked at Judge Evans, sitting there so serene, self-poised, and cold, and began to wonder if he had ever been a boy, a young man,—if Mrs. Evans ever was a girl,—if he was ever in love with her, and what he did when he was.

I thought of the lock of Emmy's hair which I had observed in John's writing-desk in days when he was falling in love with her,—of sundry little movements in which, at awkward moments, I had detected my grave and serious gentleman when I had stumbled accidentally upon the pair in moonlight strolls, or retired corners,—and wondered whether the models of propriety before me had ever been convicted of any such human weaknesses. Now, to be sure, I could as soon imagine the stately tongs to walk up and kiss the shovel as conceive of any such bygone effusion in those dignified individuals. But how did they get acquainted? how came they ever to be married?

I looked at John, and thought I saw him gradually stiffening and subsiding into the very image of his father. As near as a young fellow of twenty-five can resemble an old one of sixty-two, he was growing to be exactly like him, with the same upright carriage, the same silence and reserve. Then I looked at Emmy: she, too, was changed,—she, the wild little pet, all of whose pretty individualities were dear to us,—that little unpunctuated scrap of life's poetry, full of little exceptions referable to no exact rule, only to be tolerated under the wide score of poetic license. Now, as she sat between the two Misses Evans, I thought I could detect a bored, anxious expression on her little mobile face,—an involuntary watchfulness and self-consciousness, as if she were trying to be good on some quite new pattern. She seemed nervous about some of my jokes, and her eye went apprehensively to her mother-in-law in the corner; she tried hard to laugh and make things go merrily for me; she seemed sometimes to look an apology for me to them, and then again for them to me. For myself, I felt that perverse inclination to shock people which sometimes comes over one in such situations. I had a great mind to draw Emmy on to my knee and commence a brotherly romp with her, to give John a thump on his very upright back, and to propose to one of the Misses Evans to strike up a waltz, and get the parlour into a general whirl before the very face and eyes of propriety in the corner: but "the spirits" were too strong for me; I couldn't do it.

I remembered the innocent, saucy freedom with which Emmy used to treat her John in the days of their engagement,—the little ways, half loving, half mischievous, in which she alternately petted and domineered over him. *Now* she called him "Mr. Evans," with an anxious affectation of matronly gravity. Had they been lecturing her into these conjugal proprieties? Probably not. I felt sure, by what I now experienced in myself, that, were I to live in that family one week, all such little deviations from the one accepted pattern of propriety would fall off, like many-coloured sumach-leaves after the first hard frost. I began to feel myself slowly stiffening—my courage getting gently chilly. I tried to tell a story, but had to mangle it greatly, because I felt in the air around me that parts of it were too vernacular and emphatic; and then, as a man who is freezing makes desperate efforts to throw off the spell, and finds his brain beginning to turn, so I was beginning to be slightly insane, and was haunted with a desire to say some horribly improper or wicked thing which should start them all out of their chairs. Though never given to profane expressions, I perfectly hankered to let out a certain round, unvarnished, wicked word, which I knew would create a tremendous commotion on the surface of this enchanted mill-pond,—in fact, I was so afraid that I should make some such mad demonstration, that I rose at an early hour and begged leave to retire. Emmy sprang up with apparent relief, and offered to get my candle and marshal me to my room.

When she had ushered me into the chilly hospitality of that stately apartment, she seemed suddenly disenchanted. She sat down the candle, ran to me, fell on my neck, nestled her little head under my coat, laughing and crying, and calling me her dear old boy; she pulled my whiskers, pinched my ear, rummaged my pockets, danced round me in a sort of wild joy, stunning me with a volley of questions, without stopping to hear the answer to one of them; in short, the wild little elf of old days seemed suddenly to come back to me, as I sat down and drew her on to my knee.

"It does look so like home to see you, Chris!—dear, dear home!—and the dear old folks! There never, never was such a home!—everybody there did just what they wanted to, didn't they, Chris?—and we love each other, don't we?"

"Emmy," said I, suddenly, and very improperly, "you aren't happy here."

"Not happy!" she said, with a half-frightened look, —"what makes you say so? Oh, you are mistaken. I have everything to make me happy. I should be very unreasonable and wicked if I were not. I am very, very happy, I assure you. Of course, you know, everybody can't be like our folks at home. *That* I should not expect, you know,—people's ways are different,—but then, when you know people are so good, and all that, why, of course you must be thankful,—be happy. It's better for me to learn to control my feelings, you know, and not to give way to impulses. They are all so good here, they never give way to their feelings,—they always do right. Oh, they are quite wonderful!"

"And agreeable?" said I.

"Oh, Chris, we musn't think so much of that. They certainly aren't pleasant and easy, as people at home are; but they are never cross, they never scold, they always are good, and we oughtn't to think so much of living to be happy; we ought to think more of doing right, doing our duty, don't you think so?"

"All undeniable truth, Emmy; but, for all that, John seems stiff as a ramrod, and their front parlour is like a tomb. You musn't let them petrify him."

Her face clouded over a little.

"John is different here from what he was at our house. He has been brought up differently,—oh, entirely differently from what we were; and when he comes back into the old house, the old business, and the old place between his father and mother and sisters, he goes back into the old ways. He loves me all the same, but he does not show it in the same ways, and I must learn, you know, to take it on trust. He is *very* busy,—works hard all day, and all for me; and mother says women are unreasonable that ask any other proof of love from their husbands than what they give by working for them all the time. She never lectures me, but I know she thought I was a silly little petted child, and she told me one day how she brought up John. She never petted him; she put him away alone to sleep, from the time he was six months old; she never fed him out of his regular hours when he was a baby, no matter how much he cried; she never let him talk baby-talk, or have any baby-talk talked to him, but was very careful to make him speak all his words plain from the very first; she never encouraged him to express his love by kisses or caresses, but taught him that the only proof of love was exact obedience. I remember John's telling me of his running to her once and hugging her round the neck, when he had come in without wiping his shoes, and she took off his arms and said, 'My son, this isn't the best way to show love. I should be much better pleased to have you come in quietly and wipe your shoes than to come and kiss me when you forget to do what I say.'"

"Dreadful old jade!" said I, irreverently, being then only twenty-three.

"Now, Chris, I won't have anything to say to you, if this is the way you are going to talk," said Emily, pouting, though a mischievous gleam darted into her eyes. "Really, however, I think she carries things too far, though she is so good. I only said it to excuse John, and show how he was brought up."

"Poor fellow!" said I. "I know now why he is so hopelessly shut up, and walled up. Never a warmer heart than he keeps stowed away there, inside the fortress, with the drawbridge down and moat all round."

"They are all warm-hearted inside," said Emily. "Would you think she didn't love him? Once when he was sick, she watched with him seventeen nights without taking off her clothes; she scarcely would eat all the time: Jane told me so. She loves him better than she loves herself. It's perfectly dreadful, sometimes, to see how intense she is when anything concerns him; it's her *principle* that makes her so cold and quiet."

"And a devilish one it is!" said I.

"Chris, you are really growing wicked!"

"I use the word seriously, and in good faith," said I. "Who but the Father of Evil ever devised such plans for making goodness hateful, and keeping the most heavenly part of our nature so under lock and key, that, for the greater part of our lives, we get no use of it? Of what benefit is a mine of love burning where it warms nobody, does nothing but blister the soul within with its imprisoned heat? Love repressed grows morbid, acts in a thousand perverse ways. These three women, I'll venture to say, are living in the family here like three frozen islands, knowing as little of each other's inner life as if parted by eternal barriers of ice, —and all because a cursed principle in the heart of the mother has made her bring them up in violence to nature."

"Well," said Emmy, "sometimes I do pity Jane; she is nearest my age; and, naturally, I think she was something like me, or might have been. The other day I remember her coming in looking so flushed and ill that I couldn't help asking if she were unwell. The tears came into her eyes; but her mother looked up, in her cool, business-like way, and said, in her dry voice,—

"'Jane, what's the matter?'

"'Oh, my head aches dreadfully, and I have pains in all my limbs!'

"I wanted to jump and run to do something for her—you know at our house we feel that a sick person must be waited on; but her mother only said, in the same dry way,—

"'Well, Jane, you've probably got a cold; go into the kitchen and make yourself some good boneset tea, soak your feet in hot water and go to bed at once;' and Jane meekly departed.

"I wanted to spring and do these things for her; but it's curious, in this house I never dare offer to do anything; and mother looked at me as she went out, with a significant nod,—

"'That's always *my* way; if any of the children are sick, I never coddle them; it's best to teach them to make as light of it as possible.'"

"Dreadful!" said I.

"Yes, it is dreadful," said Emmy, drawing her breath, as if relieved that she might speak her mind; "it's dreadful to see these people, who I know love each other, living side by side and never saying a loving, tender word, never doing a little loving thing,—sick ones crawling off alone like sick animals, persisting in being alone, bearing everything alone. But I won't let them; I will insist on forcing my way into their rooms. I *would* go and sit with Jane, and pet her, and hold her hand and bathe her head, though I knew it made her horribly uncomfortable at first; but I thought she ought to learn to be petted in a Christian way when she was sick. I will kiss her, too, sometimes; though she takes it just like a cat that isn't used to being stroked, and calls me a silly girl; but I know she is getting to like it. What is the use of people's loving each other in this horridly cold, stingy, silent way? If one of them were dangerously ill now, or met with any serious accident, I know there would be no end to what the others would do for her; if one of them were to die, the others would be perfectly crushed; but it would all go inward,—drop silently down into that dark, cold, frozen well; they couldn't speak to each other; they couldn't comfort each other; they have lost the power of expression; they absolutely *can't*."

"Yes," said I, "they are like the fakirs who have held up an arm till it has become stiffened,—they cannot now change its position; like the poor mutes, who, being deaf, have become dumb through disuse of the organs of speech. Their education has been like those iron suits of armour into which little boys were put in the middle ages, solid, inflexible, put on in childhood, enlarged with every year's growth, till the warm human frame fitted the mould as if it had been melted and poured into it. A person educated in this way is hopelessly crippled, never will be what he might have been."

"Oh, don't say that, Chris; think of John; think how good he is!"

"I do think how good he is,"—with indignation,—"and how few know it, too. I think that, with the tenderest, truest, gentlest heart, the utmost appreciation of human friendship, he has passed in the world for a cold, proud, selfish man. If your frank, impulsive, incisive nature had not unlocked gates and opened doors, he would never have known the love of woman; and now he is but half disenchanted; he every day tends to go back to stone."

"But I shan't let him; oh, indeed, I know the danger! I shall bring him out. I shall work on them all. I know they are beginning to love me a good deal; in the first place, because I belong to John, and everything belonging to him is perfect; and in the second place,——"

"In the second place, because they expect to weave, day after day, the fine cobweb lines of their cold system of repression around you, which will harden and harden, and tighten and tighten, till you are as stiff and shrouded as any of them. You remind me of our poor little duck: don't you remember him?"

"Yes, poor fellow! how he would stay out, and swim round and round, while the pond kept freezing and freezing, and his swimming-place grew smaller and smaller every day; but he was such a plucky little fellow that——"

"That at last we found him one morning frozen tight in, and he has limped ever since on his poor feet."

"Oh, but I won't freeze in," she said, laughing.

"Take care, Emmy! You are sensitive, approbative,

delicately organized; your whole nature inclines you to give way and yield to the nature of those around you. One little lone duck such as you, however warm-blooded, light-hearted, cannot keep a whole pond from freezing. While you have any influence, you must use it all to get John away from these surroundings, where you can have him to yourself."

"Oh, you know we are building our house; we shall go to housekeeping soon."

"Where? Close by, under the very guns of this fortress, where all your housekeeping, all your little management, will be subject to daily inspection."

"But mamma never interferes, never advises,—unless I ask advice."

"No, but she influences; she lives, she looks, she is there; and while she is there, and while your home is within a stone's throw, the old spell will be on your husband, on your children, if you have any; you will feel it in the air; it will constrain, it will sway you, it will rule your house, it will bring up your children."

"Oh, no! never! never! I never could! I never will! If God should give me a dear little child, I will not let it grow up in these hateful ways!"

"Then, Emmy, there will be a constant, still, undefined, but real friction of your life-power, from the silent grating of your wishes and feelings on the cold, positive millstone of their opinion; it will be a life-battle with a quiet, invisible, pervading spirit, who will never show himself in fair fight, but who will be around you in the very air you breathe, at your pillow when you lie down and when you rise. There is so much in these friends of yours noble, wise, severely good,—their aims are so high, their efficacy so great, their virtues so many,—that they will act upon you with the force of a conscience, subduing, drawing, insensibly constraining you into their moulds. They have stronger wills, stronger natures than yours; and between the two forces of your own nature and theirs you will be always oscillating, so that you will never show what you can do, working either in your own way or yet in theirs: your life will be a failure."

"Oh, Chris, why do you discourage me?"

"I am trying tonic treatment, Emily; I am showing you a real danger; I am rousing you to flee from it. John is making money fast; there is no reason why he should always remain buried in this town. Use your influence as they do,—daily, hourly, constantly,—to predispose him to take you to another sphere. Do not always shrink and yield; do not conceal and assimilate and endeavour to persuade him and yourself that you are happy; do not put the very best face to him on it all; do not tolerate his relapses daily and hourly into his habitual, cold, inexpressive manner; and don't lay aside your own little impulsive, outspoken ways. Respect your own nature, and assert it; woo him, argue with him; use all a woman's weapons to keep him from falling back into the old Castle Doubting where he lived till you let him out. Dispute your mother's hateful dogma, that love is to be taken for granted without daily proof between lovers; cry down latent caloric in the market; insist that the mere fact of being a wife is not enough,—that the words spoken once, years ago, are not enough,—that love needs new leaves every summer of life, as much as your elm-trees, and new branches to grow broader and wider, and new flowers at the root to cover the ground."

"Oh, but I have heard that there is no surer way to lose love than to be exacting, and that it never comes for a woman's reproaches."

"All true as gospel, Emmy. I am not speaking of reproaches, or of unreasonable self-assertion, or of ill-temper,—you could not use any of these forces if you would, you poor little chick! I am speaking now of the highest duty we owe our friends, the noblest, the most sacred,—that of keeping their own nobleness, goodness, pure and incorrupt. Thoughtless, instinctive, unreasoning love and self-sacrifice, such as many women long to bestow on husband and children, soil and lower the very objects of their love. *You* may grow saintly by self-sacrifice; but do your husband and children grow saintly by accepting it without return? I have seen a verse which says,—

'They who kneel at woman's shrine
Breathe on it as they bow.'

Is not this true of all unreasoning love and self-devotion? If we *let* our friend become cold and selfish and exacting without a remonstrance, we are no true lover—no true friend. Any good man soon learns to discriminate between the remonstrance that comes from a woman's love to his soul, her concern for his honour, her anxiety for his moral development, and the pettish cry which comes from her own personal wants. It will be your own fault if, for lack of anything you can do, your husband relapses into these cold, undemonstrative habits which have robbed his life of so much beauty and enjoyment. These dead, barren ways of living are as unchristian as they are disagreeable; and you, as a good little Christian sworn to fight heroically under Christ's banner, must make headway against this sort of family Antichrist, though it comes with a show of superior sanctity and self-sacrifice. Remember, dear, that the Master's family had its outward tokens of love as well as its inward life. The beloved leaned on His bosom; and the traitor could not have had a sign for his treachery had there not been a daily kiss at meeting and parting with His children."

"I am glad you have said all this," said Emily, "because now I feel stronger for it. It does not now seem so selfish for me to want what it is better for John to give. Yes, I must seek what will be best for him."

And so the little one, put on the track of self-sacrifice, began to see her way clearer, as many little women of her sort do. Make them look on self-assertion as one form of martyrdom, and they will come into it.

But, for all my eloquence on this evening, the house was built in the self-same spot as projected; and the family life went on, under the shadow of Judge Evans's elms, much as if I had not spoken. Emmy became mother of two fine, lovely boys, and waxed dimmer and fainter; while with her physical decay came increasing need of the rule in the household of mamma and sisters, who took her up energetically on eagles' wings, and kept her house, and managed her children; for what can be done when a woman hovers half her time between life and death?

At last I spoke out to John, that the climate and atmosphere were too severe for her who had become so dear to him,—to them all; and then they consented that the change much talked of and urged, but always opposed by the parents, should be made.

John bought a pretty cottage in our neighbourhood, and brought his wife and boys; and the effect of change of moral atmosphere verified all my predictions. In a year we had our own blooming, joyous, impulsive little Emily once more,—full of life, full of cheer, full of energy,—looking to the ways of her household,—the merry companionship of her growing boys,—the blithe empress over her husband, who took to her genial sway as in the old happy days of courtship. The nightmare was past, and John was as joyous as any of us in his freedom. As Emmy said, he was turned right side out for life; and we all admired the pattern. And that is the end of my story.

And now for the moral,—and that is, that life consists of two parts,—*Expression* and *Repression*,—each of which has its solemn duties. To love, joy, hope, faith, pity, belongs the duty of *expression*: to anger, envy, malice, revenge, and all uncharitableness belongs the duty of *repression*.

Some very religious and moral people err by applying *repression* to both classes alike. They repress equally the expression of love and of hatred, of pity and of anger. Such forget one great law, as true in the moral world as in the physical,—that repression lessens and deadens. Twice or thrice mowing will kill off the sturdiest crop of weeds; the roots die for want of expression. A compress on a limb will stop its growing; the surgeon knows this, and puts a tight bandage around a tumour; but what if we put a tight bandage about the heart and lungs, as some young ladies of my acquaintance do,—or bandage the feet, as they do in China? And what if we bandage a nobler inner faculty, and wrap *love* in grave-clothes?

But, again, there are others, and their number is legion,—perhaps you and I, reader, may know something of it in ourselves,—who have an instinctive habit of repression in regard to all that is noblest and highest within them, which they do not feel in their lower and more unworthy nature.

It comes far easier to scold our friend, in an angry moment, than to say how much we love, honour, and esteem him, in a kindly mood. Wrath and bitterness speak themselves and go with their own force; love is shame-faced, looks shyly out of the window, lingers long at the door-latch.

How much freer utterance among many good Christians have anger, contempt, and censoriousness, than tenderness and love! *I hate* is said loud, and with all our force: *I love* is said with a hesitating voice and blushing cheek.

In an angry mood we do an injury to a loving heart with good, strong, free emphasis; but we stammer and hang back when our diviner nature tells us to confess and ask pardon. Even when our heart is broken with repentance, we haggle and linger long before we can

"Throw away the worser part of it."

How many live a stingy and niggardly life in regard to their richest inward treasures! They live with those they love dearly, whom a few more words and deeds expressive of this love would make so much happier, richer, and better; and they cannot, will not, turn the key and give it out. People who in their very souls really do love, esteem, reverence, almost worship each other, live a barren, chilly life side by side, busy, anxious, preoccupied, letting their love go by as a matter of course, a last year's growth, with no present buds and blossoms.

Are there not sons and daughters who have parents living with them as angels unawares,—husbands and wives, brothers and sisters in whom the material for a beautiful life lies locked away in unfruitful silence,—who give time to everything but the cultivation and expression of mutual love?

The time is coming, they think, in some far future, when they shall find leisure to enjoy each other, to stop and rest side by side, to discover to each other these hidden treasures which lie idle and unused.

Alas! time flies and death steals on, and we reiterate the complaint of one in Scripture,—"It came to pass, while thy servant was busy hither and thither, the man was gone."

The bitterest tears shed over graves are for words left unsaid and deeds left undone. "She never knew how I loved her!" "He never knew what he was to me!" "I always meant to make more of our friendship!" "I did not know what he was to me till he was gone!" Such words are the poisoned arrows which cruel Death shoots backward at us from the door of the sepulchre.

How much more we might make of our family life, of our friendships, if every secret thought of love blossomed into a deed! We are not now speaking merely of personal caresses. These may or may not be the best language of affection. Many are endowed with a delicacy, a fastidiousness of physical organization, which shrinks away from too much of these, repelled and overpowered. But there are words and looks and little observances, thoughtfulnesses, watchful little attentions, which make it manifest, and there is scarce a family that might not be richer in heart-wealth for more of them.

It is a mistake to suppose that relations must of course love each other because they are relations. Love must be cultivated, and can be increased by judicious culture, as wild-fruits may double their bearing under the hand of a gardener; and love can dwindle and die out by neglect, as choice flower-seeds planted in poor soil dwindle and grow single.

Two causes in our Anglo-Saxon nature prevent this easy faculty and flow of expression which strike one so pleasantly in the Italian or the French life: the dread of flattery, and a constitutional shyness.

"I perfectly longed to tell So-and-so how I admired her, the other day," says Miss X.

"And why in the world didn't you tell her?"

"Oh, it would seem like flattery, you know."

Now what is flattery?

Flattery is *insincere* praise, given from interested motives, not the sincere utterance of a friend of what we deem good and lovely in him.

And so, for fear of flattering, these dreadfully sincere people go on side by side with those they love and admire, giving them, all the time, the impression of utter indifference. Parents are so afraid of exciting pride and vanity in their children by the expression of their love and approbation, that a child sometimes goes sad and discouraged by their side, and learns with surprise, in some chance way, that they are proud and fond of him. There are times when the open expression of a father's love would be worth more than church or sermon to a boy; and his father cannot utter it,—will not show it.

The other thing that represses the utterances of love, is the characteristic *shyness* of the Anglo-Saxon blood. Oddly enough, a race born of two demonstrative, outspoken nations—the German and the French—has an habitual reserve that is like neither. There is a powerlessness of utterance in our blood that we should fight against, and struggle outward towards expression. We can educate ourselves to it, if we know and feel the necessity; we can make it a Christian duty, not only to love, but to be loving,—not only to be true friends, but to *show* ourselves friendly. We can make ourselves say the kind things that rise in our hearts and tremble on our lips,—do the gentle and helpful deeds which we long to do and shrink back from; and, little by little, it will grow easier,—the love spoken will bring back the answer of love,—the kind deed will bring back a kind deed in return,—till the hearts in the family circle, instead of being so many frozen, icy islands, shall be full of warm airs and echoing bird-voices, answering back and forth with a constant melody of love.

IV.

SELF-WILL.

MY little foxes are interesting little beasts; and I only hope my reader will not get tired of my charming menagerie, before I have done showing him their nice points. He must recollect there are seven of them, and as yet we have shown up only three; so let him have patience.

As before stated, little foxes are the little pet sins of us educated, good Christians, who hope that we have got above and far out of sight of stealing, lying, and those other gross evils against which we pray every Sunday, when the Ten Commandments are read. They are not generally considered of dignity enough to be fired at from the pulpit; they seem to us too trifling to be remembered in church; they are like the red spiders on plants,—too small for the perception of the naked eye, and only to be known by the shrivelling and dropping of leaf after leaf that ought to be green and flourishing.

I have another little fox in my eye, who is most active and most mischievous in despoiling the vines of domestic happiness,—in fact, who has been guilty of destroying more grapes than anybody knows of. His name I find it difficult to give with exactness. In my enumeration I called him *Self-Will;* another name for him—perhaps a better one—might be *Persistence.*

Like many another, this fault is the overaction of a most necessary and praiseworthy quality. The power of firmness is given to man as the very granite foundation of life. Without it, there would be nothing accomplished; all human plans would be unstable as water on an inclined plane. In every well-constituted nature there must be a power of tenacity, a gift of perseverance of will; and that man might not be without a foundation for so needful a property, the Creator has laid it in an animal faculty, which he possesses in common with the brutes.

The animal power of firmness is a brute force, a matter of brain and spinal cord, differing in different animals. The force by which a bulldog holds on to an antagonist, the persistence with which a mule will plant his four feet and set himself against blows and menaces, are good examples of the purely animal phase of a property which exists in human beings, and forms the foundation for that heroic endurance, for that perseverance, which carries on all the great and noble enterprises of life.

The domestic fault we speak of is the wild, uncultured growth of this faculty, the instinctive action of firmness uncontrolled by reason or conscience,—in common parlance, the being "*set in one's way.*" It is the *animal* instinct of being "set in one's way" which we mean by self-will or persistence; and in domestic life it does the more mischief from its working as an instinct, unwatched by reason and unchallenged by conscience.

In that pretty new cottage which you see on yonder knoll are a pair of young people just in the midst of that happy bustle which attends the formation of a first home in prosperous circumstances, and with all the means of making it charming and agreeable. Carpenters, upholsterers, and artificers await their will; and there remains for them only the pleasant task of arranging and determining where all their pretty and agreeable things shall be placed. Our Hero and Leander are decidedly nice people, who have been through all the proper stages of being in love with each other for the requisite and suitable time. They have written each other a letter every day for two years, beginning with "My dearest," and ending with "Your own," &c.; they have sent each other flowers and rings and locks of hair; they have worn each other's pictures on their hearts; they have spent hours and hours talking over all subjects under the sun, and are convinced that never was there such sympathy of souls, such unanimity of opinion, such a just, reasonable, perfect foundation for mutual esteem.

Now it is quite true that people may have a perfect agreement and sympathy in their higher intellectual nature,—may like the same books, quote the same poetry, agree in the same principles, be united in the same religion,—and nevertheless, when they come together in the simplest affair of every-day business, may find themselves jarring and impinging upon each other at every step, simply because they are to each person, in respect of daily personal habits and personal likes and dislikes, a thousand little individualities with which reason has nothing to do, which are not subjects for the use of logic, and to which they never think of applying the power of religion,—which can only be set down as the positive ultimate facts of existence with two people.

Suppose a blue jay courts and wins and weds a Baltimore oriole. During courtship there may have been delightfully sympathetic conversation on the charm of being free birds, the felicity of soaring in the blue summer air. Mr. Jay may have been all humility and all ecstasy in comparing the discordant screech of his own note with the warbling tenderness of Miss Oriole. But, once united, the two commence business relations. He is firmly convinced that a hole in a hollow tree is the only reasonable nest for a bird; she is positive that she should die there in a month of damp and rheumatism. She never heard of going to housekeeping in anything but a nice little pendulous bag, swinging down from under the branches of a breezy elm; he is sure he should have water on the brain before summer was over, from constant vertigo, in such swaying, unsteady quarters,—he would be a sea-sick blue jay on land, and he cannot think of it. She knows now he don't love her, or he never would think of shutting her up in an old mouldy hole picked out of rotten wood; and *he* knows she doesn't love him, or she never would want to make him uncomfortable all his days, by tilting and swinging him about as no decent bird ought to be swung. Both are dead-set in their own way and opinion; and how is either to be convinced that the way which seemeth right unto the other is not best? Nature knows this, and therefore, in her feathered tribes, blue jays do not mate with orioles: and so bird-housekeeping goes on in peace.

But men and women as diverse in their physical tastes and habits as blue jays and orioles are wooing and wedding every day, and coming to the business of nest-building, *alias* housekeeping, with predilections as violent, and as incapable of any logical defence, as the oriole's partiality for a swing-nest and the jay's preference of rotten wood.

Our Hero and Leander, then, who are arranging their cottage to-day, are examples just in point. They have both of them been only children,—both the idols of circles where they have been universally deferred to. Each in his or her own circle has been looked up to as a model of good taste, and of course each has the habit of exercising and indulging very distinct personal tastes. They truly, deeply esteem, respect, and love each other, and for the very best of reasons,—because there are sympathies of the very highest kind between them. Both are generous and affectionate,—both are highly cultured in intellect and taste,—both are earnestly religious; and yet, with all this, let me tell you that the first year of their married life will be worthy to be recorded as *a year of battles.* Yes, these friends so true, these lovers so ardent, these individuals in themselves so admirable, cannot come into the intimate relations of life without an effervescence as great as that of an acid and alkali; and it will be impossible to decide which is most in fault, the acid or the alkali, both being in their way of the very best quality.

The reason of it all is, that both are intensely "*set in their way*," and the ways of no two human beings are altogether coincident. Both of them have the most sharply defined, exact tastes and preferences. In the simplest matter both have *a way*,—an exact way,—which seems to be dear to them as life's blood. In the simplest appetite or taste they know exactly what they want, and cannot, by any argument, persuasion, or coaxing, be made to want anything else.

For example, this morning dawns bright upon them, as she, in her tidy morning wrapper and trimly-laced boots, comes stepping over the bales and boxes which are discharged on the verandah; while he, for joy of his new acquisition, can hardly let her walk on her own pretty feet, and is making every fond excuse to lift her over obstacles and carry her into her new dwelling in triumph.

Carpets are put down, the floors glow under the hands of obedient workmen, and now the furniture is being wheeled in.

"Put the piano in the bow-window," says the lady.

"No, not in the bow-window," says the gentleman.

"Why, my dear, of course it must go in the bow-window. How awkward it would look anywhere else! I have always seen pianos in bow-windows."

"My love, certainly you would not think of dashing that beautiful prospect from the bow-window by blocking it up with the piano. The proper place is just here, in the corner of the room. Now try it."

"My dear, I think it looks dreadfully there; it spoils the appearance of the room."

"Well, for my part, my love, I think the appearance of the room would be spoiled if you filled up the bow-window. Think what a lovely place that would be to sit in!"

"Just as if we couldn't sit there behind the piano, if we wanted to!" says the lady.

"But then, how much more ample and airy the room looks as you open the door, and see through the bow-window down that little glen, and that distant peep of the village-spire!"

"But I never could be reconciled to the piano standing in the corner in that way," says the lady. "*I insist* upon it, it ought to stand in the bow-window: it's the way mamma's stands, and Aunt Jane's, and Mrs. Wilcox's; everybody has their piano so."

"If it comes to *insisting*," says the gentleman, "it strikes me that is a game two can play at."

"Why, my dear, you know a lady's parlour is her own ground."

"Not a married lady's parlour, I imagine. I believe it is at least equally her husband's, as he expects to pass a good portion of his time there."

"But I don't think you ought to insist on an arrangement that really is disagreeable to me," says the lady.

"And I don't think you ought to insist on an arrangement that is really disagreeable to me," says the gentleman.

And now Hero's cheeks flush, and the spirit burns within, as she says,—

"Well, if you insist upon it, I suppose it must be as you say; but I shall never take any pleasure in playing on it;" and Hero sweeps from the apartment, leaving the victor very unhappy in his conquest.

He rushes after her, and finds her up-stairs, sitting disconsolate and weeping on a packing-box.

"Now, Hero, how silly! Do have it your own way. I'll give it up."

"No,—let it be as you say. I forgot that it was a wife's duty to submit."

"Nonsense, Hero! Do talk like a rational woman. Don't let us quarrel like children."

"But it's so evident that I was in the right."

"My dear, I cannot concede that you were in the right; but I am willing it should be as you say."

"Now, I perfectly wonder, Leander, that you don't see how awkward your way is. It would make me nervous every time I came into the room, and it would be so dark in that corner that I never could see the notes."

"And I wonder, Hero, that a woman of your taste don't see how shutting up that bow-window spoils the parlour. It's the very prettiest feature of the room."

And so round and round they go, stating and re-stating their arguments, both getting more and more nervous and combative, both declaring themselves perfectly ready to yield the point as an oppressive exaction, but to do battle for their own opinion as right and reason,—the animal instinct of self-will meanwhile rising and rising and growing stronger and stronger on both sides. But meanwhile in the heat of argument some side-issues and personal reflections fly out like splinters in the shivering of lances. He tells her, in his heat, that her notions are formed from deference to models in fashionable life, and that she has no idea of adaptation,—and she tells him that he is domineering and dictatorial, and wanting to have everything his own way; and in fine, this battle is fought off and on through the day, with occasional armistices of kisses and makings-up,—treacherous truces, which are all broken up by the fatal words, "My dear, after all, you must admit *I* was in the right," which, of course, is the signal to fight the whole battle over again.

One such prolonged struggle is the parent of many lesser ones,—the aforenamed splinters of injurious remark and accusation which flew out in the heat of argument, remaining and festering and giving rise to nervous soreness; yet, where there is at the foundation real, genuine love, and a good deal of it, the pleasure of making up so balances the pain of the controversy, that the two do not perceive exactly what they are doing, nor suspect that so deep and wide a love as theirs can be seriously affected by causes so insignificant.

But the cause of difficulty in both, the silent, unwatched, intense power of self-will in trifles, is all the while precipitating them into new encounters. For example, in a bright hour between the showers, Hero arranges for her Leander a repast of peace and good-will, and compounds for him a salad which is a *chef-d'œuvre* among salads. Leander is also bright and propitious; but after tasting the salad, he pushes it silently away.

"My dear, you don't like your salad."

"No, my dear; I never eat anything with salad oil in it."

"Not eat salad oil? How absurd! I never heard of a salad without oil." And the lady looks dis turbed.

"But, my dear, as I tell you, I never take it. I prefer simple sugar and vinegar."

"Sugar and vinegar! Why, Leander, I'm astonished! How very *bourgeois!* You must really try to like my salad"—(spoken in a coaxing tone).

"My dear, I *never* try to like anything new. I am satisfied with my old tastes."

"Well, Leander, I must say that is very ungracious and disobliging of you."

"Why any more than for you to annoy me by forcing on me what I don't like?"

"But you would like it, if you would only try People never like olives till they have eaten three or four, and then they become passionately fond of them."

"Then I think they are very silly to go through all that trouble, when there are enough things that they do like."

"Now, Leander, I don't think that seems amiable or pleasant at all. I think we ought to try and accommodate ourselves to the tastes of our friends."

"Then, my dear, suppose you try to like your salad with sugar and vinegar."

"But it's so *gauche* and unfashionable! Did you ever hear of a salad made with sugar and vinegar on a table in good society?"

"My mother's table, I believe, was in good society, and I learned to like it there. The truth is, Hero, for a sensible woman, you are too fond of mere fashionable and society notions."

"Yes, you told me that last week, and I think it was very unjust,—*very unjust, indeed*"—(uttered with emphasis).

"No more unjust than your telling me that I was dictatorial and obstinate."

"Well, now, Leander, dear, you must confess that you are rather obstinate."

"I don't see the proof."

"You insist on your own ways so, heaven and earth can't turn you."

"Do I insist on mine more than you on yours?"

"Certainly, you do."

"I don't think so."

Hero casts up her eyes and repeats with expression,—

> "Oh, wad some power the giftie gie us
> To see oursels as cthers see us!"

"Precisely," says Leander. "I would that prayer were answered in your case, my dear."

"I think you take pleasure in provoking me," says the lady.

"My dear, how silly and childish all this is!" says the gentleman. "Why can't we let each other alone?"

"You began it."

"No, my dear, begging your pardon, I did not."

"Certainly, Leander, you did."

Now a conversation of this kind may go on hour after hour, as long as the respective parties have breath and strength, both becoming secretly more and more "set in their way." On both sides is the consciousness that they might end it at once by a very simple concession.

She might say,—"Well, dear, you shall always have your salad as you like;" and he might say,—"My dear, I will try to like your salad, if you care much about it;" and if either of them would utter one of these sentences, the other would soon follow. Either would give up if the other would set the example; but as it is, they remind us of nothing so much as two cows that we have seen standing, with locked horns, in a meadow, who can neither advance nor recede an inch. It is a mere dead-lock of the animal instinct of firmness; reason, conscience, religion have nothing to do with it.

The questions debated in this style by our young couple were surprisingly numerous: as, for example, whether their favourite copy of Turner should hang in the parlour or in the library,—whether their pet little landscape should hang against the wall, or be placed on an easel,—whether the bust of Psyche should stand on the marble table in the hall, or on a bracket in the library; all of which points were debated with a breadth of survey, a richness of imagery, a vigour of discussion, that would be perfectly astonishing to any one who did not know how much two self-willed, argumentative people might find to say on any point under heaven. Everything in classical antiquity, everything in Kugler's "Hand-Book of Painting,"—every opinion of living artists,—besides questions social, moral, and religious,—all mingled in the grand *mêlée*: because there is nothing in creation that is not somehow connected with everything else.

Dr. Johnson has said,—"There are a thousand familiar disputes which reason never can decide; questions that elude investigation, and make logic ridiculous; cases where something must be done, and where little can be said."

With all deference to the great moralist, we must say that this statement argues a very limited knowledge of the resources of talk possessed by two very cultivated and very self-willed persons, fairly pitted against each other in practical questions; the logic may indeed be ridiculous, but such people as our Hero and Leander find no cases under the sun where something is to be done, yet where little can be said. And these wretched wranglings, this interminable labyrinth of petty disputes, waste and crumble away that high ideal of truth and tenderness, which the real, deep sympathies and actual worth of their characters entitled them to form. Their married life is not what they expected; at times they are startled by the reflection that they have somehow grown unlovely to each other; and yet, if Leander goes away to pass a week, and thinks of his Hero in the distance, he can compare no other woman to her; and the days seem long and the house empty to Hero while he is gone; both wonder at themselves when they look over their petty bickerings, but neither knows exactly how to catch the little fox that spoils their vines.

It is astonishing how much we think about ourselves, yet to how little purpose,—how very clever people will talk and wonder about themselves and each other, and yet go on year after year, not knowing how to use either themselves or each other,—not having as much practical philosophy in the matter of their own characters and that of their friends, as they have in respect of the screws of their gas-fixtures or the management of their water-pipes.

"But *I* won't have any such scenes with *my* wife," says Don Positivo. "I won't marry one of your clever women; they are always positive and disagreeable. *I* look for a wife of a gentle and yielding nature, that shall take her opinions from me, and accommodate her tastes to mine." And so Don Positivo goes and marries a pretty little pink-and-white concern, so lisping and soft and delicate that he is quite sure she cannot have a will of her own. She is the moon of his heavens, to shine only by his reflected light.

We would advise our gentlemen friends who wish to

enjoy the felicity of having their own way not to try the experiment with a pretty fool; for the obstinacy of cleverness and reason is nothing to the obstinacy of folly and inanity.

Let our friend once get in the seat opposite to him at table a pretty creature who cries for the moon, and insists that he don't love her because he doesn't get it for her; and in vain may he display his superior knowledge of astronomy, and prove to her that the moon is not to be got. She listens with her head on one side, and after he has talked himself quite out of breath, repeats the very same sentence she began the discussion with, without variation or addition.

If she wants darling Johnny taken away from school, because cruel teachers will not give up the rules of the institution for his pleasure, in vain does Don Positivo, in the most select and superior English, enlighten her on the necessity of habits of self-control and order for a boy,—the impossibility that a teacher should make exceptions for their particular darling,—the absolute, perishing need that the boy should begin to do something. She hears him all through, and then says, "I don't know anything about that. I know what I want: I want Johnny taken away." And so she weeps, sulks, storms, entreats, lies awake nights, has long fits of sick-headache,—in short, shows that a pretty animal, without reason or cultivation, can be, in her way, quite as formidable an antagonist as the most clever of her sex.

Leander can sometimes vanquish his Hero in fair

fight by the weapons of good logic, because she is a woman capable of appreciating reason, and able to feel the force of the considerations he adduces; and when he does vanquish and carry her captive by his bow and spear, he feels that he has gained a victory over no ignoble antagonist, and he becomes a hero in his own eyes. Though a woman of much will, still she is a woman of much reason; and if he has many vexations with her pertinacity, he is never without hope in her good sense; but alas for him whose wife has only the animal instinct of firmness, without any development of the judgment or reasoning faculties! The conflicts with a woman whom a man respects and admires are often extremely trying; but the conflicts with one whom he cannot help despising, become in the end simply disgusting.

But the inquiry now arises, What shall be done with all the questions Dr. Johnson speaks of, which reason cannot decide, which elude investigation, and make logic ridiculous,—cases where something must be done, and where little can be said?

Read Mrs. Ellis's "Wives of England," and you have one solution of the problem. The good women of England are there informed that there is to be no discussion, that everything in the *ménage* is to follow the rule of the lord, and that the wife has but one hope, namely, that grace may be given him to know exactly what his own will is. "*L'état, c'est moi,*" is the lesson which every English husband learns of Mrs. Ellis, and we should judge from the pictures of English novels that this "awful right divine" is insisted on in detail in domestic life.

Miss Edgeworth makes her magnificent General Clarendon talk about his "commands" to his accomplished and elegant wife; and he rings the parlour-bell with such an air, calls up and interrogates trembling servants with such awful majesty, and lays about him generally in so very military and tremendous a style, that we are not surprised that poor little Cecilia is frightened into lying, being half out of her wits in terror of so very martial a husband.

During his hours of courtship he majestically informs her mother that he never could consent to receive as *his* wife any woman who has had another attachment; and so the poor puss, like a naughty girl, conceals a little school-girl flirtation of bygone days, and thus gives rise to most agonizing and tragic scenes with her terrible lord, who petrifies her one morning by suddenly drawing the bed-curtains and flapping an old love-letter in her eyes, asking, in tones of suppressed thunder, "Cecilia, is this your writing?"

The more modern female novelists of England give us representations of their view of the right divine no less stringent. In a very popular story, called "Agatha's Husband," the plot is as follows. A man marries a beautiful girl with a large fortune. Before the marriage, he discovers that his brother, who has been guardian of the estate, has fraudulently squandered the property, so that it can only be retrieved by the strictest economy. For the sake of getting her heroine into a situation to illustrate her moral, the authoress now makes her hero give a solemn promise not to divulge to his wife or to any human being the fraud by which she suffers.

The plot of the story then proceeds to show how very badly the young wife behaves when her husband takes her to mean lodgings, deprives her of wonted luxuries and comforts, and obstinately refuses to give any kind of sensible reason for his conduct. Instead of looking up to him with blind faith and unquestioning obedience, following his directions without inquiry, and believing not only without evidence, but against apparent evidence, that he is the soul of honour and wisdom, this perverse Agatha murmurs, complains, thinks herself very ill-used, and occasionally is even wicked enough, in a very mild way, to say so,—whereat her husband looks like a martyr and suffers in silence; and thus we are treated to a volume of mutual distresses, which are at last ended by the truth coming out, the abused husband mounting the throne in glory, and the penitent wife falling in the dust at his feet, and confessing what a wretch she has been all along to doubt him.

The authoress of "Jane Eyre" describes the process of courtship in much the same terms as one would describe the breaking of a horse. Shirley is contumacious and self-willed, and Moore, her lover and tutor, gives her "*Le Cheval dompté*" for a French lesson, as a gentle intimation of the work he has in hand in paying her his addresses; and after long struggling against his power, when at last she consents to his love, he addresses her thus, under the figure of a very fierce leopardess:—

" Tame or wild, fierce or subdued, you are *mine*."

And she responds:—

" I am glad I know my keeper and am used to him. Only his voice will I follow, only his hand shall manage me, only at his feet will I repose."

The accomplished authoress of " Nathalie " represents the struggles of a young girl engaged to a man far older than herself, extremely dark and heroic, fond of behaving in a very unaccountable manner, and declaring, nevertheless, in very awful and mysterious tones, that he has such a passion for being believed in, that if any one of his friends, under the most suspicious circumstances, admits *one doubt* of his honour, all will be over between them for ever.

After establishing his power over Nathalie fully, and amusing himself quietly for a time with the contemplation of her perplexities and anxieties, he at last unfolds to her the mysterious counsels of his will by declaring to another of her lovers, in her presence, that he " has the intention of asking this young lady to become his wife." During the engagement, however, he contrives to disturb her tranquillity by insisting prematurely on the right divine of husbands, and, as she proves fractious, announces to her that, much as he loves her, he sees no prospect of future happiness in their union, and that they had better part.

The rest of the story describes the struggles and anguish of the two, who pass through a volume of distresses, he growing more cold, proud, severe, and misanthropic than ever, all of which is supposed to be the fault of naughty Miss Nathalie, who might have made a saint of him, could she only have found her highest pleasure in letting him have his own way. Her conscience distresses her; it is all her fault; at last, worn out in the strife, she resolves to be a good girl, goes to his library, finds him alone, and, in spite of an insulting reception, humbles herself at his feet, gives up all her naughty pride, begs to be allowed to wait on him as a handmaid, and is rewarded by his graciously announcing, that, since she will stay with him at all events, she *may* stay as his wife; and the story leaves her in the last sentence sitting in what we are informed is the only true place of happiness for a woman, at her husband's feet.

This is the solution which the most cultivated women of England give of the domestic problem, according to these fair interpreters of English ideas.

The British lion on his own domestic hearth, standing in awful majesty with his back to the fire and his hands under his coat-tails, can be supposed to have no such disreputable discussions as we have described; since his partner, as Miss Bronté says, has learned to know her keeper, and her place at his feet, and can conceive no happiness so great as hanging the picture and setting the piano exactly as he likes.

Of course this will be met with a general shriek of horror on the part of our fair republican friends, and an equally general disclaimer on the part of our American gentlemen, who, so far as we know, would be quite embarrassed by the idea of assuming any such pronounced position at the fireside.

The genius of American institutions is not towards a display of authority. All needed authority exists among us, but exists silently, with as little external manifestation as possible.

Our President is but a fellow-citizen, personally the equal of other citizens. We obey him because we have chosen him, and because we find it convenient, in regulating our affairs, to have one final appeal and one deciding voice.

The position in which the Bible and the Marriage Service place the husband in the family amounts to no more. He is the head of the family in all that relates to its material interests, its legal relations, its honour and standing in society; and no true woman who respects herself would any more hesitate to promise to yield to him this position and the deference it implies, than an officer of State to yield to the President. But because the President is officially above Mr. Seward, it does not follow that there can be nothing between them but absolute command on the one part, and prostrate submission on the other; neither does it follow that the superior claims in all respects to regulate the affairs and conduct of the inferior. There are still wide spheres of individual freedom, as there are in the case of husband and wife; and no sensible man but would feel himself ridiculous in entering another's proper sphere with the voice of authority.

The inspired declaration, that "the husband is the head of the wife, even as Christ is the head of the Church," is certainly to be qualified by the evident points of difference in the subjects spoken of. It certainly does not mean that any man shall be invested with the rights of omnipotence and omniscience, but simply that in the family state he is the head and protector, even as the Saviour is in the Church. It is merely the announcement of a great natural law of society which obtains through all the tribes and races of men,—a great and obvious fact of human existence.

The silly and senseless reaction against this idea in some otherwise sensible women is, I think, owing to the kind of extravagances and overstatements to which we have alluded. It is as absurd to cavil at the word *obey* in the marriage ceremony, as for a military officer to set himself against the etiquette of the army, or a man to refuse the freeman's oath.

Two young men every way on a footing of equality and friendship may be one of them a battalion-commander and the other a staff-officer. It would be alike absurd for the one to take airs about not obeying a man every way his equal, and for the other to assume airs of lordly dictation out of the sphere of his military duties. The mooting of the question of marital authority between two well-bred, well-educated Christian people of the nineteenth century is no less absurd.

While the husband has a certain power confided to him for the support and maintenance of the family, and for the preservation of those relations which involve its good name and well-being before the world, he has no claim to an authoritative exertion of will in reference to the little personal tastes and habits of the interior. He has no divine right to require that everything shall be arranged to please him, at the expense of his wife's preferences and feelings, any more than if he were not the head of the household. In a thousand indifferent matters, which do not touch the credit and respectability of the family, he is just as much bound, sometimes to give up his own will and way for the comfort of his wife as she is in certain other matters to submit to his decisions. In a large number of cases the husband and wife stand as equal human beings before God, and the indulgence of unchecked and inconsiderate self-will on either side is a sin.

It is my serious belief that writings such as we have been considering do harm both to men and women, by insensibly inspiring in the one an idea of a licensed prerogative of selfishness and self-will, and in the other an irrational and indiscreet servility.

Is it any benefit to a man to find in the wife of his bosom the flatterer of his egotism, the acquiescent victim of his little selfish exactions, to be nursed and petted and cajoled in all his faults and fault-findings, and to see everybody falling prostrate before his will in the domestic circle? Is this the true way to make him a manly and Christ-like man? It is my belief that many so-called good wives have been accessory to making their husbands very bad Christians.

However, then, the little questions of difference in every-day life are to be disposed of between two individuals, it is in the worst possible taste and policy to undertake to settle them by mere authority. All romance, all poetry, all beauty are over forever with a couple between whom the struggle of mere authority has begun. No, there is no way out of difficulties of this description but by the application, on both sides, of good sense and religion to the little differences of life.

A little reflection will enable any person to detect in himself that setness in trifles which is the result of the unwatched instinct of self-will, and to establish over himself a jealous guardianship.

Every man and every woman, in their self-training and self-culture, should study the art of giving up with a good grace. The charm of polite society is formed by that sort of freedom and facility in all the members of a circle which makes each one pliable to the influences of the others, and sympathetic to slide into the moods and tastes of others without a jar.

In courteous and polished circles there are no stiff railroad-tracks, cutting straight through everything, and grating harsh thunders all along their course, but smooth, meandering streams, tranquilly bending hither and thither to every undulation of the flowery banks. What makes the charm of polite society would make no less the charm of domestic life; but it can come only by watchfulness and self-discipline in each individual.

Some people have much more to struggle with in this way than others. Nature has made them precise and exact. They are punctilious in their hours, rigid in their habits, pained by any deviation from regular rule.

Now Nature is always perversely ordering that men

and women of just this disposition should become desperately enamoured of their exact opposites. The man of rules and formulas and hours has his heart carried off by a gay, careless little chit, who never knows the day of the month, tears up the newspaper, loses the door-key, and makes curl-papers out of the last bill; or, *per contra*, our exact and precise little woman, whose belongings are like the waxen cells of a bee, gives her heart to some careless fellow, who enters her sanctum in muddy boots, upsets all her little nice household divinities whenever he is going on a hunting or fishing bout, and can see no manner of sense in the discomposure she feels in the case.

What can such couples do, if they do not adopt the compromises of reason and sense,—if each arms his or her own peculiarities with the back force of persistent self-will, and runs them over the territories of the other?

A sensible man and woman, finding themselves thus placed, can govern themselves by a just philosophy, and, instead of carrying on a life-battle, can modify their own tastes and requirements, turn their eyes from traits which do not suit them to those which do, resolving, at all events, however reasonable be the taste or propensity which they sacrifice, to give up all rather than have domestic strife.

There is one form which persistency takes that is peculiarly trying: I mean that persistency of opinion which deems it necessary to stop and raise an argument in self-defence, on the slightest personal criticism.

John tells his wife that she is half an hour late with her breakfast this morning, and she indignantly denies it.

"But look at my watch!"

"Your watch isn't right."

"I set it by railroad time."

"Well, that was a week ago; that watch of yours always gains."

"No, my dear, you're mistaken."

"Indeed I'm not. Did I not hear you telling Mr. B—— about it?"

"My dear, that was a year ago,—before I had it cleaned."

"How can you say so, John? It was only a month ago."

"My dear, you are mistaken."

And so the contest goes on, each striving for the last word.

This love of the last word has made more bitterness in families, and spoiled more Christians than it is worth. A thousand little differences of this kind would drop to the ground if either party would let them drop. Suppose John is mistaken in saying breakfast is late,—suppose that fifty of the little criticisms which we make on one another are well or ill-founded, are they worth a discussion? Are they worth ill-tempered words, such as are almost sure to grow out of a discussion? Are they worth throwing away peace and love for? Are they worth the destruction of the only fair ideal left on earth,—a quiet, happy home? Better let the most unjust statements pass in silence than risk one's temper in a discussion upon them.

Discussions, assuming the form of warm arguments, are never pleasant ingredients of domestic life—never safe recreations between near friends. They are, generally speaking, mere unsuspected vents for self-will; and the cases are few where they do anything more than to make both parties more positive in their own way than they were before.

A calm comparison of opposing views, a fair statement of reasons on either side, may be valuable; but when warmth and heat and love of victory and pride of opinion come in, good temper and good manners are too apt to step out.

And now Christopher, having come to the end of his subject, pauses for a sentence to close with. There are a few lines of a poet that sum up so beautifully all he has been saying that he may be pardoned for closing with them:—

"Alas! how light a cause may move
Dissension between hearts that love;
Hearts that the world has vainly tried,
And sorrow but more closely tied;
That stood the storm when waves were rough,
Yet in a sunny hour fall off,
Like ships that have gone down at sea
When heaven was all tranquillity!
A something light as air, a look,
A word unkind, or wrongly taken,—
Oh, love that tempests never shook,
A breath, a touch like this hath shaken!
For ruder words will soon rush in
To spread the breach that words begin,

And eyes forget the gentle ray
They wore in courtship's smiling day,
And voices lose the tone which shed
A tenderness round all they said,—
Till, fast declining, one by one,
The sweetnesses of love are gone,
And hearts, so lately mingled, seem
Like broken clouds, or like the stream,
That, smiling, left the mountain-brow
As though its waters ne'er could sever,
Yet, ere it reaches the plain below,
Breaks into floods that part for ever."

V.

INTOLERANCE.

"AND what are you going to preach about this month, Mr. Crowfield?"

"I am going to give a sermon on *Intolerance*, Mrs. Crowfield."

"Religious intolerance?"

"No,—domestic and family and educational intolerance,—one of the seven deadly sins on which I am preaching,—one of 'the foxes.'"

People are apt to talk as if all the intolerance in life were got up and expended in the religious world; whereas religious intolerance is only a small branch of the radical, strong, all-pervading intolerance of human nature.

Physicians are quite as intolerant as theologians. They never have had the power of burning at the stake for medical opinions, but they certainly have shown the will. Politicians are intolerant. Philosophers are intolerant, especially those who pique themselves on liberal opinions. Painters and sculptors are intolerant. And housekeepers are intolerant, virulently denunciatory concerning any departures from their particular domestic creed.

Mrs. Alexander Exact, seated at her domestic altar,

gives homilies on the degeneracy of modern housekeeping equal to the lamentations of Dr. Holdfast as to the falling off from the good old faith.

"Don't tell me about pillow-cases made without felling," says Mrs. Alexander; "it's slovenly and shiftless. I wouldn't have such a pillow-case in my house any more than I'd have vermin."

"But," says a trembling young housekeeper, conscious of unfelled pillow-cases at home, "don't you think, Mrs. Alexander, that some of these old traditions might be dispensed with? It really is not necessary to do all the work that has been done so thoroughly and exactly, —to double-stitch every wristband, fell every seam, count all the threads of gathers, and take a stitch to every gather. It makes beautiful sewing, to be sure; but when a woman has a family of little children and a small income, if all her sewing is to be kept up in this perfect style, she wears her life out in stitching. Had she not better slight a little, and get air and exercise?"

"Don't tell me about air and exercise! What did my grandmother do? Why, she did all her own work and made grandfather's ruffled shirts besides, with the finest stitching and gathers; and she found exercise enough, I warrant you. Women of this day are miserable, sickly, degenerate creatures."

"But, my dear Madam, look at poor Mrs. Evans, over the way, with her pale face and her eight little ones."

"Miserable manager," said Mrs. Alexander. "If she'd get up at five o'clock the year round, as I do, she'd find time enough to do things properly, and be the better for it."

"But, my dear Madam, Mrs. Evans is a very delicately organized, nervous woman."

"Nervous! Don't tell me! Every woman now-a-days is nervous. She can't get up in the morning, because she's nervous. She can't do her sewing decently, because she's nervous. Why, I might have been as nervous as she is, if I'd have petted and coddled myself as she does. But I get up early, take a walk in the fresh air of a mile or so before breakfast, and come home feeling the better for it. I do all my own sewing,—never put out a stitch; and I flatter myself my things are made as they ought to be. I always make my boy's shirts and Mr. Exact's, and they are made as shirts ought to be,—and yet I find plenty of time for calling, shopping, business, and company. It only requires management and resolution."

"It is perfectly wonderful, to be sure, Mrs. Exact, to see all that you do; but don't you get very tired sometimes?"

"No, not often. I remember, though, the week before last Christmas, I made and baked eighteen pies and ten loaves of cake in one day, and I was really quite worn out; but I didn't give way to it. I told Mr. Exact I thought it would rest me to take a drive into New York and attend the Sanitary Fair, and so we did. I suppose Mrs. Evans would have thought she must go to bed and coddle herself for a month."

"But, dear Mrs. Exact, when a woman is kept awake nights by crying babies——"

"There's no need of having crying babies: my babies never cried; it's just as you begin with children. I might have had to be up and down every hour of the night with mine, just as Mrs. Evans is; but I knew better. I used to take 'em up about ten o'clock, and feed and make 'em all comfortable; and that was the last of 'em, till I was ready to get up in the morning. I never lost a night's sleep with any of mine."

"Not when they were teething?"

"No. I knew how to manage that. I used to lance their gums myself, and I never had any trouble: it's all in management. I weaned 'em all myself, too: there's no use in having any fuss in weaning children."

"Mrs. Exact, you are a wonderful manager; but it would be impossible to bring up all babies so."

"You'll never make me believe that: people only need to begin right. I'm sure I've had a trial of eight."

"But there's that one baby of Mrs. Evans's makes more trouble than all your eight. It cries every night so that somebody has to be up walking with it; it wears out all the nurses, and keeps poor Mrs. Evans sick all the time."

"Not the least need of it; nothing but shiftless management. Suppose I had allowed my children to be walked with; I might have had terrible times, too; but I began right. I set down my foot that they should lie still, and they did; and if they cried, I never lighted a candle, or took 'em up, or took any kind of notice of it; and so, after a little, they went off to sleep. Babies very soon find out where they can take advantage, and where they can't. It's nothing but temper makes babies cry; and if I couldn't hush 'em any other way, I should give 'em a few good smart slaps, and they would soon learn to behave themselves."

"But, dear Mrs. Exact, you were a strong healthy woman, and had strong healthy children."

"Well, isn't that baby of Mrs. Evans's healthy, I want to know? I'm sure it is a great creature, and thrives and grows fat as fast as ever I saw a child. You needn't tell me anything is the matter with that child but temper, and its mother's coddling management."

Now, in the neighbourhood where she lives, Mrs. Alexander Exact is the wonderful woman, the Lady Bountiful, the pattern female. Her cake never rises on one side, or has a heavy streak in it. Her furs never get a moth in them; her carpets never fade; her sweetmeats never ferment; her servants never neglect their work; her children never get things out of order; her babies never cry, never keep one awake o'nights; and her husband never in his life said, "My dear, there's a button off my shirt." Flies never infest her kitchen, cockroaches and red ants never invade her premises, a spider never had time to spin a web on one of her walls. Everything in her establishment is shining with neatness, crisp and bristling with absolute perfection,—and it is she, the ever-up-and-dressed, unsleeping, wide-awake, omnipresent, never-tiring Mrs. Exact, that does it all.

Besides keeping her household ways thus immaculate, Mrs. Exact is on all sorts of charitable committees, does all sorts of fancy-work for fairs; and whatever she does is done perfectly. She is a most available, most helpful, most benevolent woman, and general society has reason to rejoice in her existence.

But, for all this, Mrs. Exact is as intolerant as Torquemada or a locomotive engine. She has her own track, straight and inevitable; her judgments and opinions cut through society in right lines, with all the force of her example and all the steam of her energy, turning out neither for the old nor the young, the weak nor the weary. She cannot, and she will not, conceive the possibility that there may be other sorts of natures than her own, and that other kinds of natures must have other ways of living and doing.

Good and useful as she is, she is terrible as an army with banners to her poor, harassed, delicate, struggling neighbour, across the way, who, in addition to an aching, confused head, an aching back, sleepless, harassed nights, and weary, sinking days, is burdened everywhere and every hour with the thought that Mrs. Exact thinks all her troubles are nothing but poor management, and that she might do just like her, if she would. With very little self-confidence or self-assertion, she is withered and paralyzed with this discouraging thought. *Is* it, then, her fault that this never-sleeping baby cries all night, and that all her children never could and never would be brought up by those exact rules which she hears of as so efficacious in the household over the way? The thought of Mrs. Alexander Exact stands over her like a constable; the remembrance of her is grievous; the burden of her opinion is heavier than all her other burdens.

Now the fact is, that Mrs. Exact comes of a long-lived, strong-backed, strong-stomached race, with "limbs of British oak and nerves of wire." The shadow of a sensation of nervous pain or uneasiness never has been known in her family for generations, and her judgments of poor little Mrs. Evans are about as intelligent as those of a good stout Shanghai hen on a humming-bird. Most useful and comfortable, these Shanghai hens,—and very ornamental, and in a small way useful, these humming-birds; but let them not regulate each other's diet, or lay down schemes for each other's housekeeping. Has not one as much right to its nature as the other?

This intolerance of other people's natures is one of the greatest causes of domestic unhappiness. The perfect householders are they who make their household rule so flexible that all sorts of differing natures may find room to grow and expand and express themselves without infringing upon others.

Some women are endowed with a tact for understanding human nature and guiding it. They give a sense of largeness and freedom; they find a place for every one, see at once what every one is good for, and are inspired by nature with the happy wisdom of not wishing or asking of any human being, more than that human being was made to give. They have the portion in due season for all: a bone for the dog; cat-nip for the cat; cuttle-fish and hemp-seed for the bird; a book or review for their bashful literary visitor; lively gossip for thoughtless Miss Seventeen; knitting for Grandmamma; fishing-rods, boats, and gunpowder for Young Restless, whose beard is just beginning to grow; —and they never fall into pets because the canary-bird won't relish the dog's bone, or the dog eat canary-seed, or young Miss Seventeen read old Mr. Sixty's review, or young Master Restless take delight in knitting-work, or old Grandmamma feel complacency in guns and gunpowder.

Again, there are others who lay the foundations of family life so narrow, straight, and strict, that there is room in them only for themselves and people exactly like themselves; and hence comes much misery.

A man and woman come together out of different families and races, often united by only one or two sympathies, with many differences. Their first wisdom would be to find out each other's nature, and accommodate to it as a fixed fact; instead of which, how many spend their lives in a blind fight with an opposite nature, as good as their own in its way, but not capable of meeting their requirements!

A woman trained in an exact, thriving, business family, where her father and brothers carried on everything with true worldly skill and energy, falls in love with a literary man, who knows nothing of such affairs, whose life is in his library and his pen. Shall she vex and torment herself and him because he is not a business man? Shall she constantly hold up to him the example of her father and brothers, and how they would manage in this and that case? or shall she say cheerily and once for all to herself,—"My husband has no talent for business; that is not his forte; but then he has talents far more interesting: I cannot have everything; let him go on undisturbed, and do what he can do well, and let me try to make up for what he cannot do; and if difficulties come on us in consequence of what we neither of us can do, let us both take them cheerfully?"

In the same manner a man takes out of the bosom of an adoring family one of those delicate, petted singing-birds that seem to be created simply to adorn life and make it charming. Is it fair, after he has got her, to compare her housekeeping, and her efficiency and capability in the material part of life, with those of his mother and sisters, who are strong-limbed, practical women, that have never thought about anything but housekeeping from their cradle? Shall he all the while vex himself and her with the remembrance of how his mother used to get up at five o'clock and arrange all the business of the day,—how she kept all the accounts,—how she saw to everything and settled everything,—how there never were break-downs or irregularities in her system?

This would be unfair. If a man wanted such a housekeeper, why did he not get one? There were plenty of single women who understood washing, ironing, clear-starching, cooking, and general housekeeping, better than the little canary-bird which he fell in love with, and wanted for her plumage and her song—for her merry tricks, for her bright eyes and pretty ways. Now he has got his bird, let him keep it as something fine and precious, to be cared for and watched over, and treated according to the laws of its frail and delicate nature; and so treating it, he may many years keep the charms which first won his heart. He may find, too, if he watches and is careful, that a humming-bird can, in its own small, dainty way, build a nest as efficiently as a turkey-gobbler, and hatch her eggs and bring up her young in humming-bird fashion; but to do it she must be left unfrightened and undisturbed.

But the evils of domestic intolerance increase with the birth of children. As parents come together out of different families with ill-assorted peculiarities, so children are born to them with natures differing from their own and from each other.

The parents seize on their first new child as a piece of special property which they are forthwith to turn to their own account. The poor little waif, just drifted on the shores of Time, has perhaps folded up in it a character as positive as that of either parent; but, for all that, its future course is marked out for it—all arranged and predetermined.

John has a perfect mania for literary distinction. His own education was somewhat imperfect, but he is determined his children shall be prodigies. His first-born turns out a girl, who is to write like Madame de Staël,—to be an able, accomplished woman. He bores her with literature from her earliest years, reads extracts from Milton to her when she is only eight years old and is secretly longing to be playing with her doll's wardrobe. He multiplies governesses, spares no expense, and when, after all, his daughter turns out to be only a very pretty, sensible, domestic girl, fond of cross-stitching embroidery, and with a more decided vocation for sponge-cake and pickles than for poetry and composition, he is disappointed and treats her coldly; and she is unhappy and feels that she has vexed her parents, because she cannot be what nature never meant her to be. If John had taken meekly the present that Mother Nature gave him, and humbly set himself to inquire what it was, and what it was good for, he might have had years of happiness with a modest, amiable, and domestic daughter, to whom had been given the instinct to study household good.

But, again, a bustling, pickling, preserving, stocking-knitting, universal-housekeeping woman has a daughter who dreams over her knitting-work, and hides a book under her sampler,—whose thoughts are straying in Greece, Rome, Germany,—who is reading, studying, thinking, writing, without knowing why; and the mother sets herself to fight this nature, and to make the dreamy scholar into a driving, thorough-going, exact woman of business. How many tears are shed, how much temper wasted, how much time lost in such encounters!

Each of these natures, under judicious training, might be made to complete itself by cultivation of that which it lacked. The born housekeeper can never be made a genius, but she may add to her household virtues some reasonable share of literary culture and appreciation,—and the born scholar may learn to come down out of her clouds, and see enough of this earth to walk its practical ways without stumbling; but this must be done by tolerance of their nature,—by giving it play and room,—first recognizing its existence and its rights, and then seeking to add to it the properties it wants.

A driving Yankee housekeeper, fruitful of resources, can work with any tools or with no tools at all. If she absolutely cannot get a tack-hammer with a claw on one end, she can take up carpet-nails with an iron spoon, and drive them down with a flat-iron; and she has sense enough not to scold, though she does her work with them at considerable disadvantage. She knows that she is working with tools made to do something else, and never thinks of being angry at their unhandiness. She might have equal patience with a daughter unhandy in physical things, but acute and skilful in mental ones, if she once had the idea suggested to her.

An ambitious man has a son whom he destines to a learned profession. He is to be the Daniel Webster of the family. The boy has a robust, muscular frame—great physical vigour and enterprise—a brain bright and active in all that may be acquired through the bodily senses, but which is dull and confused and wandering when put to abstract book-knowledge. He knows every ship at the wharf, her build, tonnage, and sailing qualities; he knows every railroad-engine, its power, speed, and hours of coming and going; he is always busy, sawing, hammering, planing, digging, driving, making bargains, with his head full of plans, all relating to something outward and physical. In all these matters his mind works strongly, his ideas are clear, his observation acute, his conversation sensible and worth listening to. But as to the distinction between common nouns and proper nouns, between the subject and the predicate of a sentence, between the relative pronoun and the demonstrative adjective pronoun, between the perfect and the preter-perfect tense, he is extremely dull and hazy. The region of abstract ideas is to him a region of ghosts and shadows. Yet his youth is mainly a dreary wilderness of uncomprehended, incomprehensible studies, of privations, tasks, punishments, with a sense of continual failure, disappointment, and disgrace, because his father is trying to make a scholar and a literary man out of a boy whom Nature made to till the soil or manage the material forces of the world. He might be a farmer, an engineer, a pioneer of a new settlement, a sailor, a soldier, a thriving man of business; but he grows up feeling that his nature is a crime, and that he is good for nothing, because he is not good for what he had been blindly predestined to before he was born.

Another boy is a born mechanic; he understands machinery at a glance: he is always pondering and studying and experimenting. But his wheels and his axles and his pulleys are all swept away, as so much irrelevant lumber; he is doomed to go into the Latin School, and spend three or four years in trying to learn what he never can learn well,—disheartened by always being at the tail of his class, and seeing many a boy inferior to himself in general culture, who is rising to brilliant distinction simply because he can remember those hopeless, bewildering Greek quantities and accents which he is constantly forgetting,—as, for example, how properispomena become paroxytones when the ultimate becomes long, and proparoxytones become paroxytones when the ultimate becomes long, while paroxytones with a short penult remain paroxytones. Each of this class of rules, however, having about sixteen exceptions, which hold good except in three or four other exceptional cases under them, the labyrinth becomes delightfully wilder and wilder; and the crowning beauty of the whole is, that when the bewildered boy has swallowed the whole, —tail, scales, fins, and bones,—he then is allowed to read the classics in peace, without the slightest occasion to refer to them again during his college course.

The great trouble with the so-called classical course of education is, that it is made strictly but for one class of minds, which it drills in respects for which they have by nature an aptitude, and to which it presents scarcely enough of difficulty to make it a mental discipline, while to another and equally valuable class of minds it presents difficulties so great as actually to crush and discourage. There are, we will venture to say, in every ten boys in Boston four, and those not the dullest or poorest in quality, who could never go through the discipline of the Boston Latin School without such a strain on the brain and nervous system as would leave them no power for anything else.

A bright, intelligent boy, whose talents lay in the line of natural philosophy and mechanics, passed with brilliant success through the Boston English High School. He won the first medals, and felt all that pride and enthusiasm which belong to a successful student. He entered the Latin Classical School. With a large philosophic and reasoning brain, he had a very poor verbal and textual memory; and here he began to see himself distanced by boys who had hitherto looked up to him. They could rattle off catalogues of names; they could do so all the better from the habit of not thinking of what they studied. They could commit to memory the Latin Grammar, large print and small, and run through the interminable mazes of Greek accents and inflections. This boy of large mind and brain, always behindhand, always incapable, utterly discouraged, no amount of study could place on an equality with his former inferiors. His health failed, and he dropped from school. Many a fine fellow has been lost to himself, and lost to an educated life, by just such a failure. The collegiate system is like a great coal-screen: every piece not of a certain size must fall through. This may do well enough for screening coal; but what if it were used indiscriminately for a mixture of coal and diamonds?

"Poor boy!" said Ole Bull, compassionately, when one sought to push a schoolboy from the steps of an omnibus, where he was getting a surreptitious ride. "Poor boy! let him stay. Who knows his trials? Perhaps he studies Latin!"

The witty Heinrich Heine says, in bitter remembrance of his early sufferings,—"The Romans would never have conquered the world if they had had to learn their own language. They had leisure, because they were born with the knowledge of what nouns form their accusatives in *im*."

Now we are not among those who decry the Greek and Latin classics. We think it a glorious privilege to read both those grand old tongues, and that an intelligent, cultivated man who is shut out from the converse of the splendid minds of those olden times, loses a part of his birthright; and therefore it is that we mourn that but one dry, hard, technical path, one sharp, straight, narrow way, is allowed into so goodly a land of knowledge. We think there is no need that the study of Greek and Latin should be made such a horror. There is many a man without a verbal memory, who could neither recite in order the paradigms of the Greek verbs, nor repeat the lists of nouns that form their accusative in one termination or another, who, nevertheless, by the exercise of his faculties of comparison and reasoning, could learn to read the Greek and Latin classics so as to take their sense and enjoy their spirit; and that is all that they are worth caring for. We have known one young scholar, who could not by any possibility repeat the lists of exceptions to the rules in the Latin Grammar, who yet delightedly filled his private note-book with quotations from the "Æneid," and was making extracts of literary gems from his Greek Reader, at the same time that he was every day "screwed" by his tutor upon some technical point of the language.

Is there not many a master of English, many a writer and orator, who could not repeat from memory the list of nouns ending in *y* that form their plural in *ies*, with the exceptions under it? How many of us could do this? Would it help a good writer and fluent speaker to know the whole of Murray's Grammar by heart, or does real knowledge of a language ever come in this way?

At present the rich stores of ancient literature are kept like the savory stew which poor Dominie Sampson heard simmering in the witch's kettle. One may have much appetite, but there is but one way of getting it. The Meg Merrilies of our educational system, with her harsh voice, and her "Gape, sinner, and swallow," is the only introduction,—and so, many a one turns and runs frightened from the feast.

This intolerant mode of teaching the classical languages is peculiar to them alone. Multitudes of girls and boys are learning to read and to speak German, French, and Italian, and to feel all the delights of expatiating in the literature of a new language, purely because of a simpler, more natural, less pedantic mode of teaching these languages.

Intolerance in the established system of education works misery in families, because family pride decrees that every boy of good status in society—will he, nill he

—shall go through college, or he almost forfeits his position as a gentleman.

"Not go to Cambridge!" says Scholasticus to his first-born. "Why, I went there,—and my father, and his father, and his father before him. Look at the Cambridge Catalogue and you will see the names of our family ever since the college was founded!"

"But I can't learn Latin and Greek," says young Scholasticus. "I can't remember all those rules and exceptions. I've tried and I can't. If you could only know how my head feels when I try! And I won't be at the foot of the class all the time, if I have to get my living by digging."

Suppose, now, the boy is pushed on at the point of the bayonet to a kind of knowledge in which he has no interest, communicated in a way that requires faculties which Nature has not given him,—what occurs?

He goes through his course, either shamming, shirking, parrying, all the while consciously discredited and dishonoured,—or else putting forth an effort that is a draft on all his nervous energy, he makes merely a decent scholar, and loses his health for life.

Now, if the principle of toleration were once admitted into classical education,—if it were admitted that the great object is to read and enjoy a language, and the stress of the teaching were placed on the few things absolutely essential to this result,—if the tortoise were allowed time to creep, and the bird permitted to fly, and the fish to swim, towards the enchanted and divine sources of Helicon,—all might in their own way arrive there, and rejoice in its flowers, its beauty, and its coolness.

"But," say the advocates of the present system, "it is good mental discipline."

I doubt it. It is mere waste of time.

When a boy has learned that in the genitive plural of the first declension of Greek nouns the final syllable is circumflexed, but to this there are the following exceptions: 1. That feminine adjectives and participles in *-ος, -η, -ον* are accented like the genitive masculine, but other feminine adjectives and participles are perispomena in the genitive plural; 2. That the substantives *chrestes*, *aphue*, *etesiai*, and *chlounes* in the genitive plural remain paroxytones (Kühner's *Elementary Greek Grammar*, p. 22),—I say, when a boy has learned this and twenty other things just like it, his mind has not been one whit more disciplined than if he had learned the list of the old thirteen States, the number and names of the newly-adopted ones, the times of their adoption, and the population, commerce, mineral and agricultural wealth of each. These, too, are merely exercises of memory, but they are exercises in what is of some interest and some use.

The particulars above cited are of so little use in understanding the Greek classics that I will venture to say that there are intelligent English scholars who have never read anything but Bohn's translations, who have more genuine knowledge of the spirit of the Greek mind, and the peculiar idioms of the language, and more enthusiasm for it, than many a poor fellow who has stumbled blindly through the originals with the bayonet of the tutor at his heels, and his eyes and ears full of the Scotch snuff of the Greek Grammar.

What then? Shall we not learn these ancient tongues? By all means. "So many times as I learn a language, so many times I become a man," said Charles V.; and he said rightly. Latin and Greek are foully belied by the prejudices created by this technical, pedantic mode of teaching them, which makes one ragged, prickly bundle of all the dry facts of the language, and insists upon it that the boy shall not see one glimpse of its beauty, glory, or interest, till he has swallowed and digested the whole mass. Many die in this wilderness, with their shoes worn out before reaching the Promised Land of Plato and the Tragedians.

"But," say our college authorities, "look at England. An English school-boy learns three times the Latin and Greek that our boys learn, and has them well drubbed in."

And English boys have three times more beef and pudding in their constitution than American boys have, and three times less of nerves. The difference of nature must be considered here; and the constant influence flowing from English schools and universities must be tempered by considering who we are, what sort of boys we have to deal with, what treatment they can bear, and what are the needs of our growing American society.

The demands of actual life, the living, visible facts of practical science, in so large and new a country as ours, require that the ideas of the ancients should be given us in the shortest and most economical way possible, and that scholastic technicalities should be reserved to those whom Nature made with especial reference to their preservation.

On no subject is there more intolerant judgment, and more suffering from such intolerance, than on the much-mooted one of the education of children.

Treatises on education require altogether too much of parents, and impose burdens of responsibility on tender spirits which crush the life and strength out of them. Parents have been talked to as if each child came to them a soft, pulpy mass, which they were to pinch and pull and pat and stroke into shape quite at their leisure,—and a good pattern being placed there before them, they were to proceed immediately to set up and construct a good human being in conformity therewith.

It is strange that believers in the divine inspiration of the Bible should have entertained this idea, overlooking the constant and affecting declaration of the great Heavenly Father that *He* has nourished and brought up children and they have rebelled against Him, together with His constant appeals,—"What could have been done more to my vineyard that I have not done in it? Wherefore, when I looked that it should bring forth grapes, brought it forth wild grapes?" If even God—wiser, better, purer, more loving—admits Himself baffled in this great work, is it expedient to say to human beings that the forming power, the deciding force, of a child's character is in their hands?

Many a poor feeble woman's health has been strained

to breaking, and her life darkened, by the laying on her shoulders of a burden of responsibility that never ought to have been placed there; and many a mother has been hindered from using such powers as God has given her, because some preconceived mode of operation has been set up before her which she could no more make effectual than David could wear the armour of Saul.

A gentle, loving, fragile creature marries a strong-willed, energetic man, and, by the laws of natural descent, has a boy given to her of twice her amount of will and energy. She is just as helpless, in the mere struggle of will and authority, with such a child, as she would be in a physical wrestle with a six-foot man.

What then? Has Nature left her helpless for her duties? Not if she understands her nature, and acts in the line of it. She has no power of command, but she has power of persuasion. She can neither bend nor break the boy's iron will, but she can melt it. She has tack to avoid the conflict in which she would be worsted. She can charm, amuse, please, and make willing; and her fine and subtile influences, weaving themselves about him day after day, become more and more powerful. Let her alone, and she will have her boy yet.

But now some bustling mother-in-law or other privileged expounder says to her,—

"My dear, it's your solemn duty to break that boy's will. I broke my boy's will short off. Keep your whip in sight, meet him at every turn, fight him whenever he crosses you, never let him get one victory, and finally his will will be wholly subdued."

Such advice is mischievous, because what it proposes is as utter an impossibility to the woman's nature as for a cow to scratch up worms for her calf, or for a hen to suckle her chickens.

There are men and women of strong, resolute will who are gifted with the power of governing the wills of others. Such persons can govern in this way,—and their government, being in the line of their nature, acting strongly, consistently, naturally, makes everything move harmoniously. Let them be content with their own success, but let them not set up as general education-doctors, or apply their experience to all possible cases.

Again, there are others, and among them some of the loveliest and purest natures, who have no power of command. They have sufficient tenacity of will as respects their own course, but have no compulsory power over the wills of others. Many such women have been most successful mothers, when they followed the line of their own natures, and did not undertake what they never could do.

Influence is a slower acting force than authority. It seems weaker, but in the long run it often effects more. It always does better than mere force and authority without its gentle modifying power.

If a mother is high-principled, religious, affectionate, if she never uses craft or deception, if she governs her temper and sets a good example, let her hold on in good hope, though she cannot produce the discipline of a man-of-war in her noisy little flock, or make all move as smoothly as some other women to whom God has given another and different talent; and let her not be discouraged, if she seem often to accomplish but little in that great work of forming human character, wherein the great Creator of the world has declared Himself at times baffled.

Family tolerance must take great account of the stages and periods of development and growth in children.

The passage of a human being from one stage of development to another, like the sun's passage across the equator, frequently has its storms and tempests. The change to manhood and womanhood often involves brain, nerves, body, and soul in confusion; the child sometimes seems lost to himself and his parents,—his very nature changing. In this sensitive state come restless desires, unreasonable longings, unsettled purposes; and the fatal habit of indulgence in deadly stimulants, ruining all the life, often springs from the cravings of this transition period.

Here must come in the patience of the saints. The restlessness must be soothed, the family hearth must be tolerant enough to keep there the boy, whom Satan will receive and cherish if his mother does not. The male element sometimes pours into a boy, like the tides in the Bay of Fundy, with tumult and tossing. He is noisy, vociferous, uproarious, and seems bent only on disturbance; he despises conventionalities, he hates parlours, he longs for the woods, the sea, the converse of rough men, and kicks at constraint of all kinds.

Have patience now, let love have its perfect work, and in a year or two, if no deadly physical habits set in, a quiet, well-mannered gentleman will be evolved. Meanwhile, if he does not wipe his shoes, and if he will fling his hat upon the floor, and tear his clothes, and bang and hammer and shout, and cause general confusion in his belongings, do not despair; if you only get your son, the hat and clothes and shoes and noise and confusion do not matter. Any amount of toleration that keeps a boy contented at home is treasure well expended at this time of life.

One thing not enough reflected on is, that in this transition period between childhood and maturity the heaviest draft and strain of school education occurs. The boy is fitting for the university, the girl going through the studies of the college senior year, and the brain-power, which is working almost to the breaking-point to perfect the physical change, has the additional labour of all the drill and discipline of school.

The girl is growing into a tall and shapely woman, and the poor brain is put to it to find enough phosphate of lime, carbon, and other what not to build her fair edifice. The bills flow in upon her thick and fast; she pays out hand over hand: if she had only her woman to build, she might get along, but now come in demands for algebra, geometry, music, language, and the poor brain-bank stops payment; some part of the work is shabbily done, and a crooked spine or weakened lungs are the result.

Boarding-schools, both for boys and girls, are for the

most part composed of young people in this most delicate, critical portion of their physical, mental, and moral development, whose teachers are expected to put them through one straight, severe course of drill, without the slightest allowance for the great physical facts of their being. No wonder they are difficult to manage, and that so many of them drop, physically, mentally, and morally halt and maimed. It is not the teacher's fault; he but fulfils the parent's requisition, which dooms his child without appeal to a certain course, simply because others have gone through it.

Finally, as my sermon is too long already, let me end with a single reflection. Every human being has some handle by which he may be lifted, some groove in which he was meant to run; and the great work of life, as far as our relations with each other are concerned, is to lift each one by his own proper handle, and run each one in his own proper groove.

VI.

DISCOURTEOUSNESS.

"FOR my part," said my wife, "I think one of the greatest destroyers of domestic peace is Discourtesy. People neglect, with their nearest friends, those refinements and civilities which they practise with strangers."

"My dear Madam, I am of another opinion," said Bob Stephens. "The restraints of etiquette, the formalities of ceremony, are beauteous enough in out-door life; but when a man comes home, he wants leave to take off his tight boots and gloves, wear the gown and slippers, and speak his mind freely without troubling his head where it hits. Home life should be the communion of people who have learned to understand each other, who allow each other a generous latitude and freedom. One wants one place where he may feel at liberty to be tired or dull or disagreeable without ruining his character. Home is the place where we should expect to live somewhat on the credit which a full knowledge of each other's goodness and worth inspires; and it is not necessary for intimate friends to go every day through those civilities and attentions which they practise with strangers, any more than it is necessary, among literary people, to repeat the alphabet over every day before one begins to read."

"Yes," said Jennie, "when a young gentleman is paying his addresses, he helps a young lady out of a carriage so tenderly, and holds back her dress so adroitly, that not a particle of mud gets on it from the wheels; but when the mutual understanding is complete, and the affection perfect, and she is his wife, he sits still and holds the horse, and lets her climb out alone. To be sure, when pretty Miss Titmouse is visiting them, he still shows himself gallant, flies from the carriage, and holds back *her* dress: that's because he doesn't love her nor she him, and they are *not* on the ground of mutual affection. When a gentleman is only engaged, or a friend, if you hem him a cravat, or mend his gloves, he thanks you in the blandest manner; but when you are once sure of his affection, he only says, 'Very well; now I wish you would look over my shirts, and mend that rip in my coat,—and be sure you don't forget it, as you did yesterday.' For all which reasons," said Miss Jennie, with a toss of her pretty head, "I mean to put off marrying as long as possible, because I think it far more agreeable to have gentlemen friends with whom I stand on the ground of ceremony and politeness than to be restricted to one who is living on the credit of his affection. I don't want a man who gapes in my face, reads a newspaper all breakfast-time while I want somebody to talk to, smokes cigars all the evening, or reads to himself when I should like him to be entertaining, and considers his affection for me as his right and title to make himself generally disagreeable. If he has a bright face, and pleasant, entertaining, gallant ways, I like to be among the ladies who may have the benefit of them, and should take care how I lost my title to it by coming with him on the ground of domestic affection."

"Well, Miss Jennie," said Bob, "it isn't merely our sex who are guilty of making themselves less agreeable after marriage. Your dapper little fairy creatures, who dazzle us so with wondrous and fresh toilettes, who are so trim and neat and sprightly and enchanting, what becomes of them after marriage? If *he* reads the newspaper at the breakfast-table, perhaps it's because there is a sleepy, dowdy woman opposite, in a faded gingham wrapper, put on in the sacredness of domestic privacy, and perhaps she has laid aside those crisp, sparkling, bright little sayings and doings that used to make it impossible to look at or listen to anybody else when she was about. Such things are, sometimes, among the goddesses, I believe. Of course, Marianne and I know nothing of these troubles; we, being a model pair, sit among the clouds and speculate on all these matters as spectators merely."

"Well, you see what your principle leads to, carried out," said Jennie. "If home is merely the place where one may feel at liberty to be tired or dull or disagreeable, without losing one's character, I think women have far more right to avail themselves of the liberty than men; for all the lonesome, dull, disagreeable part of home-life comes into their department. It is they who must keep awake with the baby, if it frets; and if they do not feel spirits to make an attractive toilette in the morning, or have not the airy, graceful fancies that they had when they were girls, it is not so very much against them. A housekeeper and nursery-maid cannot be expected to be quite as elegant in her toilette and as entertaining in her ways as a girl without a care in her father's house; but I think that this is no excuse for husbands neglecting the little civilities and attentions which they used to show before marriage. They are strong and well and hearty; go out into the world and hear and see a great deal that keeps their minds moving and awake; and they ought to entertain their wives after marriage just as their wives entertained them before. That's the way my husband must do, or I will never have one,—and it will be small loss, if I don't," said Miss Jennie.

"Well," said Bob, "I must endeavour to initiate Charley Sedley in time."

"Charley Sedley, Bob!" said Jennie, with crimson indignation. "I wonder you will always bring up that old story, when I've told you a hundred times how disagreeable it is! Charley and I are good friends, but——"

"There, there," said Bob, "that will do; you don't need to proceed further."

"You only said that because you couldn't answer my argument," said Jennie.

"Well, my dear," said Bob, "you know everything has two sides to it, and I'll admit that you have brought up the opposite side to mine quite handsomely; but for all that, I am convinced that, if what I said was not really the truth, yet the truth lies somewhere in the vicinity of it. As I said before, so I say again, true love ought to beget freedom which shall do away with the necessity of ceremony, and much may and ought to be tolerated, among our near and dear friends, that would be discourteous among strangers. I am just as sure of this as of anything in the world."

"And yet," said my wife, "there is certainly truth in the much quoted lines of Cowper, on Friendship, where he says,—

"As similarity of mind,
Or something not to be defined,
First fixes our attention,
So manners decent and polite,
The same we practised at first sight,
Will save it from declension."

"Well, now," said Bob, "I've seen enough of French politeness between married people. When I was in Paris, I remember, there was in our boarding-house a Madame de Villiers, whose husband had conferred upon her his name and the *de* belonging to it, in consideration of a snug little income which she brought to him by the marriage. His conduct towards her was a perfect model of all the graces of civilized life. It was true that he lived on her income, and spent it promenading the Boulevards, and visiting theatres and operas with divers fair friends of easy morals; still all this was so courteously, so politely, so diplomatically arranged with Madame, that it was quite worth while to be neglected and cheated for the sake of having the thing done in so finished and elegant a manner, according to his showing. Monsieur had taken the neat little apartment for her in our *pension*, because his circumstances were embarrassed, and he would be in despair to drag such a creature into hardships which he described as terrific, and which he was resolved, heroically, to endure alone No, while a sous remained to them, his adored Julie should have her apartment and the comforts of life secured to her, while the barest attic should suffice for him. Never did he visit her without kissing her hand with the homage due to a princess, complimenting her on her good looks, bringing bonbons, entertaining her with most ravishing small-talk of all the interesting *on-dits* in Paris; and these visits were more particularly frequent as the time for receiving her quarterly instalments approached. And so Madame adored him, and could refuse him nothing, believed all his stories, and was well content to live on a fourth of her own income for the sake of so engaging a husband."

"Well," said Jennie, "I don't know to what purpose your anecdote is related, but to me it means simply this: if a rascal without heart, without principle, without any good quality, can win and keep a woman's heart merely by being invariably polite and agreeable while in her presence, how much more might a man of sense and principle and real affection do by the same means. I'm sure, if a man who neglects a woman, and robs her of her money, nevertheless keeps her affections, merely because whenever he sees her he is courteous and attentive, it certainly shows that courtesy stands for a great deal in the matter of love."

"With foolish women," said Bob.

"Yes, and with sensible ones too," said my wife. "Your Monsieur presents a specimen of the French way of doing a bad thing; but I know a poor woman whose husband did the same thing in English fashion, without kisses or compliments. Instead of flattering, he swore at her, and took her money away without the ceremony of presenting bonbons; and I assure you, if the thing must be done at all, I would, for my part much rather have it done in the French than the English manner. The courtesy, as far as it goes, is a good, and far better than nothing,—though, of course, one would rather have substantial good with it. If one must be robbed, one would rather have one's money wheedled away agreeably, with kisses and bonbons, than be knocked down and trampled upon."

"The mistake that is made on this subject," said I, "is in comparing, as people generally do, a polished rascal with a boorish good man; but the polished rascal should be compared with the polished good man, and the boorish rascal with the boorish good man and then we get the true value of the article.

"It is true as a general rule, that those races of men that are most distinguished for outward urbanity and courtesy are the least distinguished for truth and sincerity; and hence the well-known alliterations, 'fair and false,' 'smooth and slippery.' The fair and false Greek, the polished and wily Italian, the courteous and deceitful Frenchman, are associations which, to the strong, downright, courageous Anglo-Saxon, make up-and-down rudeness and blunt discourteousness a mark of truth and honesty.

"No one can read French literature without feeling how the element of courteousness pervades every department of life,—how carefully people avoid being personally disagreeable in their intercourse. A domestic quarrel, if we may trust French plays, is carried on with all the refinements of good breeding, and insults are given with elegant civility. It seems impossible to translate into French the direct and downright brutalities which the English tongue allows. The whole intercourse of life is arranged on the understanding that all personal contacts shall be smooth and civil, and such as to obviate the necessity of personal jostle and jar.

"Does a Frenchman engage a clerk or other *employé*, and afterwards hear a report to his disadvantage, the last thing he would think of would be to tell a downright unpleasant truth to the man. He writes him a civil note, and tells him, that, in consequence of an unexpected change of business, he shall not need an assistant in that department, and much regrets that this will deprive him of Monsieur's agreeable society, &c.

"A more striking example cannot be found of this sort of intercourse than the representation in the life of Madame George Sand, of the proceedings between her father and his mother. There is all the romance of affection between this mother and son. He writes her the most devoted letters, he kisses her hand on every page, he is the very image of a gallant, charming, loveable son, while at the same time he is secretly making arrangements for a private marriage with a woman of low rank and indifferent reputation,—a marriage which he knows would be like death to his mother. He marries, lives with his wife, has one or two children by her, before he will pain the heart of his adored mother by telling her the truth. The adored mother suspects her son, but no trace of the suspicion appears in her letters to him. The question which an English parent would level at him point-blank, she is entirely too delicate to address to her dear Maurice; but she puts them to the Prefect of Police, and ferrets out the marriage through legal documents, while yet no trace of this knowledge dims the affectionateness of her letters, or the serenity of her reception of her son when he comes to bestow on her the time which he can spare from his family cares. In an English or American family there would have been a battle royal, an open rupture; whereas this courteous son and mother go on for years with this polite drama, she pretending to be deceived while she is not, and he supposing that he is sparing her feelings by the deception.

"Now it is the reaction from such a style of life on the truthful Anglo-Saxon nature that leads to an undervaluing of courteousness, as if it were of necessity opposed to sincerity. But it does not follow, because all is not gold that glitters, that nothing that glitters is gold, and because courteousness and delicacy in personal intercourse are often perverted to deceit, that they are not valuable allies of truth. No woman would prefer a slippery, plausible rascal to a rough, unceremonious honest man; but of two men equally truthful and affectionate, every woman would prefer the courteous one."

"Well," said Bob, "there is a loathsome, sickly stench of cowardice and distrust about all this kind of French delicacy that is enough to drive an honest fellow to the other extreme. True love ought to be a robust, hardy plant, that can stand a free out-door life of sun and wind and rain. People who are too delicate and courteous ever fully to speak their minds to each other are apt to have stagnant residuums of unpleasant feelings, which breed all sorts of gnats and mosquitoes. My rule is, Say everything out as you go along; have your little tiffs, and get over them; jar and jolt and rub a little, and learn to take rubs and bear jolts.

"If I take less thought and use less civility of expression, in announcing to Marianne that her coffee is roasted too much, than I did to old Mrs. Pollux when I boarded with her, it's because I take it Marianne is somewhat more a part of myself than old Mrs. Pollux was,—that there is an intimacy and confidence between us which will enable us to use the short-hand of life,—that she will not fall into a passion or fly into hysterics, but will merely speak to cook in good time. If I don't thank her for mending my glove in just the style that I did when I was a lover, it is because now she does that sort of thing for me so often that it would be a downright bore to her to have me always on my knees about it. All that I could think of to say about her graceful handiness and her delicate needle-work has been said so often, and is so well understood, that it has entirely lost the zest of originality. Marianne and I have had sundry little battles, in which the victory came out on both sides, each of us thinking the better of the other for the vigour and spirit with which we conducted matters; and our habit of perfect plain-speaking and truth-telling to each other is better than all the delicacies that ever were hatched up in the hot-bed of French sentiment."

"Perfectly true, perfectly right," said I. "Every word good as gold. Truth before all things; sincerity before all things: pure, clear, diamond-bright sincerity is of more value than the gold of Ophir: the foundation of all love must rest here. How those people do who live in the nearest and dearest intimacy with friends who they believe will lie to them for any purpose, even the most refined and delicate, is a mystery to me. If I once know that my wife or my friend will tell me only what they think will be agreeable to me, then I am at once lost—my way is a pathless quicksand. But all this being premised, I still say that we Anglo-Saxons might improve our domestic life if we would graft upon the strong stock of its homely sincerity, the courteous graces of the French character.

"If anybody wishes to know exactly what I mean by this, let him read the Memoir of De Tocqueville, whom I take to be the representative of the French ideal man; and certainly the kind of family life which his domestic letters disclose has a delicacy and a beauty which adorn its solid worth.

"What I have to say on this matter is, that it is very dangerous for any individual man or any race of men continually to cry up the virtues to which they are constitutionally inclined, and to be constantly dwelling with reprobation on faults to which they have no manner of temptation.

"I think that we of the English race may set it down as a general rule that we are in no danger of becoming hypocrites in domestic life through an extra sense of politeness, and are in some danger of becoming boors from a rough, uncultivated instinct of sincerity. But to bring the matter to a practical point, I will specify some particulars in which the courtesy we show to strangers might with advantage be grafted into our home-life.

"In the first place, then, let us watch our course when we are entertaining strangers whose good opinion we wish to propitiate. We dress ourselves with care, we study what it will be agreeable to say, we do not suffer our natural laziness to prevent our being very alert in paying small attentions, we start across the room for an easier chair, we stoop to pick up the fan, we search for the mislaid newspaper, and all this for persons in whom we have no particular interest beyond the passing hour; while, with those friends whom we love and respect, we sit in our old faded habiliments, and let them get their own chair, and look up their own newspaper, and fight their own way daily, without any of this preventing care.

"In the matter of personal adornment, especially, there are a great many people who are chargeable with the same fault that I have already spoken of, in reference to household arrangements. They have a splendid wardrobe for company, and a shabby and sordid one for domestic life. A woman puts all her income into party-dresses, and thinks anything will do to wear at home. All her old tumbled finery, her frayed, dirty silks and soiled ribbons, are made to do duty for her hours of intercourse with her dearest friends. Some seem to be really principled against wearing a handsome dress in every-day life; they 'cannot afford' to be well-dressed in private. Now what I should recommend would be, to take the money necessary for one or two party-dresses and spend it upon an appropriate and tasteful home-toilette, and to make it an avowed object to look prettily at home.

"We men are a sort of stupid, blind animals: we know when we are pleased, but we don't know what it is that pleases us; we say we don't care anything about flowers, but if there is a flower-garden under our window, somehow or other, we are dimly conscious of it, and feel that there is something pleasant there; and so when our wives and daughters are prettily and tastefully attired, we know it, and it gladdens our life far more than we are, perhaps, aware of."

"Well, papa," said Jennie, "I think men ought to take just as much pains to get themselves up nicely after marriage as women. I think there are such things as tumbled shirt-collars and frowzy hair and muddy shoes, brought into the domestic sanctuary, as well as frayed silks and dirty ribbons."

"Certainly," I said; "but you know we are the natural Hottentot, and you are the missionaries who are to keep us from degenerating; we are the clumsy, old, blind Vulcan, and you the fair Cytherea, the bearers of the magic cestus, and therefore it is *to* you that this head more particularly belongs.

"Now I maintain that in family-life there should be an effort not only to be neat and decent in the arrangement of our person, but to be also what the French call *coquette*,—or to put it in plain English, there should be an endeavour to make ourselves look handsome in the eyes of our dearest friends.

"Many worthy women, who would not for the world be found wanting in the matter of personal neatness, seem somehow to have the notion that any study of the arts of personal beauty in family-life is, unmatronly; they buy their clothes with simple reference to economy, and have them made up without any question of becomingness; and hence marriage sometimes transforms a charming, trim, tripping young lady into a waddling matron whose every-day toilette suggests only the idea of a feather-bed tied round with a string. For my part, I do not believe that the summary banishment of the Graces from the domestic circle, as soon as the first baby makes its appearance, is at all conducive to domestic affection. Nor do I think that there is any need of so doing. These good housewives are in danger, like other saints, of falling into the error of neglecting the body through too much thoughtfulness for others and too little for themselves. If a woman ever had any attractiveness, let her try and keep it, setting it down as one of her domestic talents. As for my erring brothers who violate the domestic sanctuary by tousled hair, tumbled linen, and muddy shoes, I deliver them over to Miss Jennie without benefit of clergy.

"My second head is, that there should be in family-life the same delicacy in the avoidance of disagreeable topics, that characterizes the intercourse of refined society among strangers.

"I do not think that it makes family-life more sincere, or any more honest, to have the members of a domestic circle feel a freedom to blurt out in each other's faces, without thought or care, all the disagreeable things that may occur to them: as, for example, 'How horridly you look this morning! What's the matter with you?' —'Is there a pimple coming on your nose? or what is that spot?'—'What made you buy such a dreadfully unbecoming dress? It sets like a witch! Who cut it?' —'What makes you wear that pair of old shoes?'— 'Holloa, Bess! is that your party-rig? I should think you were going out for a walking advertisement of a flower-store!'—Observations of this kind between husbands and wives, brothers and sisters, or intimate friends, do not indicate sincerity, but obtuseness; and the person who remarks on the pimple on your nose is, in many cases, just as apt to deceive you as the most accomplished Frenchwoman who avoids disagreeable topics in your presence.

"Many families seem to think that it is a proof of family union and good-nature that they can pick each other to pieces, joke on each other's feelings and infirmities, and treat each other with a general tally-ho-ing rudeness, without any offence or ill-feeling. If there is a limping sister, there is a never-failing supply of jokes on 'Dot-and-go-one;' and so with other defects and peculiarities of mind or manners. Now the perfect good-nature and mutual confidence which allow all this liberty are certainly admirable; but the liberty itself is far from making home-life interesting or agreeable.

"Jokes upon personal or mental infirmities, and a general habit of saying things in jest which would be the height of rudeness if said in earnest, are all habits which take from the delicacy of family affection.

"In all this rough playing with edge-tools, many are hit and hurt who are ashamed or afraid to complain. And, after all, what possible good or benefit comes from it? Courage to say disagreeable things, when it is necessary to say them for the highest good of the person addressed, is a sublime quality; but a careless habit of saying them, in the mere freedom of family intercourse, is certainly as great a spoiler of the domestic vines as any fox running.

"There is one point under this head, which I enlarge upon for the benefit of my own sex,—I mean table-criticisms. The conduct of housekeeping, in the present state of domestic service, certainly requires great allowance; and the habit of unceremonious comment on the cooking and appointments of the table, in which some husbands habitually indulge, is the most unpardonable form of domestic rudeness. If a wife has philosophy enough not to mind it, so much the worse for her husband, as it confirms him in an unseemly habit, embarrassing to guests and a bad example to children. If she has no feelings that he is bound to respect, he should at least respect decorum and good taste, and confine the discussion of such matters to private intercourse, and not initiate every guest and child into the grating and greasing of the wheels of the domestic machinery.

"Another thing, in which families might imitate the politeness of strangers, is a wise reticence with regard to the asking of questions and the offering of advice.

"A large family includes many persons of different tastes, habits, modes of thinking and acting, and it would be wise and well to leave to each one that measure of freedom in these respects, which the laws of general politeness require. Brothers and sisters may love each other very much, and yet not enough to make joint-stock of all their ideas, plans, wishes, schemes, friendships. There are in every family circle individuals whom a certain sensitiveness of nature inclines to quietness and reserve; and there are very well-meaning families where no such quietness or reserve is possible. Nobody can be let alone, nobody may have a secret, nobody can move in any direction, without a host of inquiries and comments. 'Whom is your letter from? Let's see.'—'My letter is from So-and-so.'—*He* writing to you? I didn't know that. What's he writing about?'—'Where did you go yesterday? What did you buy? What did you give for it? What are you going to do with it?'—'Seems to me that's an odd way to do. I shouldn't do so.'—'Look here, Mary; Sarah's going to have a dress of silk tissue this spring. Now I think they're too dear,—don't you?'

"I recollect seeing in some author a description of a true gentleman, in which, among other traits, he was characterized as the man that asks the fewest questions. This trait of refined society might be adopted into home-life in a far greater degree than it is, and make it far more agreeable.

"If there is perfect unreserve and mutual confidence, let it show itself in free communications coming unsolicited. It may fairly be presumed, that, if there is anything our intimate friends wish us to know, they will tell us of it,—and that when we are on close and confidential terms with persons, and there are topics on which they do not speak to us, it is because, for some reason, they prefer to keep silence concerning them; and the delicacy that respects a friend's silence is one of the charms of life.

"As with the asking of questions, so with the offering of advice, there should be among friends a wise reticence.

"Some families are always calling each other to account at every step of the day. 'What did you put on that dress for? Why didn't you wear that?'—'What did you do this for? Why didn't you do that?'—'Now

I should advise you to do thus and so.'—And these comments and criticisms and advices are accompanied with an energy of feeling that makes it rather difficult to disregard them.

"Now it is no matter how dear and how good our friends may be, if they abridge our liberty and fetter the free exercise of our life, it is inevitable that we shall come to enjoying ourselves much better where they are not, than where they are; and one of the reasons why brothers and sisters or children so often diverge from the family circle in the choice of confidants is, that extraneous friends are bound by certain laws of delicacy not to push inquiries, criticisms, or advice too far.

"Parents would do well to remember in time when their children have grown up into independent human beings, and use with a wise moderation those advisory and admonitory powers with which they guided their earlier days. Let us give everybody a right to live his own life, as far as possible, and avoid imposing our own peculiarities on another.

"If I were to picture a perfect family, it should be a union of people of individual and marked character, who, through love, have come to a perfect appreciation of each other, and who so wisely understand themselves and one another, that each may move freely along his or her own track without jar or jostle,—a family where affection is always sympathetic and receptive, but never inquisitive,—where all personal delicacies are respected, —and where there is a sense of privacy and seclusion in following one's own course, unchallenged by the watchfulness of others, yet withal a sense of society and support in a knowledge of the kind dispositions and interpretations of all around.

"In treating of family discourtesies, I have avoided speaking of those which come from ill-temper and brute selfishness, because these are sins more than mistakes. An angry person is generally impolite; and where contention and ill-will are, there can be no courteousness. What I have mentioned are rather the lackings of good and often admirable people, who merely need to consider in their family-life a little more of whatsoever things are lovely. With such the mere admission of anything to be pursued as a duty secures the purpose; only in their somewhat earnest pursuit of the substantials of life, they drop and pass by the little things that give it sweetness and perfume. To such, a word is enough, and that word is said."

VII.

EXACTINGNESS.

AT length I am arrived at my seventh fox,—the last of the domestic quadrupeds against which I have vowed a crusade; and here opens the chase of him. I call him—

EXACTINGNESS.

And having done this, I drop the metaphor, for fear of chasing it beyond the rules of graceful rhetoric, and shall proceed to define the trait.

All the other domestic faults of which I have treated have relation to the manner in which the ends of life are pursued; but this one is an underlying, false, and diseased state of conception as to the very ends and purposes of life itself.

If a piano is tuned to exact concert pitch, the majority of voices must fall below it; for which reason most people indulgently allow their pianos to be tuned a little below this point, in accommodation to the average compass of the human voice. Persons of only ordinary powers of voice would be considered absolute monomaniacs, who should insist on having their pianos tuned to accord with any abstract notion of propriety or perfection,—rendering themselves wretched by persistently singing all their pieces miserably out of tune in consequence.

Yet there are persons who keep the requirements of life strained up always at concert pitch, and are thus worn out and made miserable all their days by the grating of a perpetual discord.

There is a faculty of the human mind to which phrenologists have given the name of *ideality*, which is at the foundation of this exactingness. Ideality is the faculty by which we conceive of and long for perfection; and at a glance it will be seen, that, so far from being an evil ingredient of human nature, it is the one element of progress that distinguishes man's nature from that of the brute. While animals go on from generation to generation, learning nothing and forgetting nothing, practising their small circle of the arts of life no better and no worse from year to year, man is driven by ideality to constant invention and alteration, whence come arts, sciences, and the whole progress of society. Ideality induces discontent with present attainments, possessions, and performances, and hence come better and better ones. So in morals, ideality constantly incites to higher and nobler modes of living and thinking, and is the faculty to which the most effective teachings of the great Master of Christianity are addressed. To be dissatisfied with present attainments, with earthly things and scenes, to aspire and press on to something for ever fair, yet for ever receding before our steps,—this is the teaching of Christianity, and the work of the Christian.

But every faculty has its own instinctive, wild growth, which, like the spontaneous produce of the earth, is crude and weedy.

Revenge, says Lord Bacon, is a sort of wild justice, obstinacy is untutored firmness,—and so exactingness is untrained ideality; and a vast deal of misery, social and domestic, comes, not of the faculty, but of its untrained exercise.

The faculty, which is ever conceiving and desiring something better and more perfect, must be modified in its action by good sense, patience, and conscience, or it induces a morbid, discontented spirit, which courses through the veins of individual and family-life like a subtle poison.

In a certain neighbourhood are two families whose social and domestic *animus* illustrates the difference between ideality and the want of it.

The Daytons are a large, easy-natured, joyous race, hospitable, kindly, and friendly.

Nothing about their establishment is much above mediocrity. The grounds are tolerably kept, the table is tolerably fair, the servants moderately good, and the family character and attainments of the same average level.

Mrs. Dayton is a decent housekeeper, and so her bread be not sour, her butter not frowy, the food abundant, and the table-cloth and dishes clean, she troubles her head little with the niceties and refinements of the *ménage*.

She accepts her children as they come from the

hand of Nature, simply opening her eyes to discern what they *are*, never raising the query what she would have had them,—forming no very high expectations concerning them, and well content with whatever develops.

A visitor in the family can easily see a thousand defects in the conduct of affairs, in the management of the children, and in this, that, and the other department of the household arrangements; but he can see and feel, also, a perfect comfortableness in the domestic atmosphere that almost atones for any defects. He can see that in a thousand respects things might be better done, if the family were not perfectly content to have them as they are, and that each individual member might make higher attainments in various directions, were there not such entire satisfaction with what is already attained.

Trying each other by very moderate standards and measurements, there is great mutual complacency. The eldest boy does not get an appointment in college,—they never expected he would; but he was a respectable scholar, and they receive him with acclamations such as another family would bestow on a valedictorian. The daughters do not profess, as we are told, to draw like artists, but some very moderate performances in the line of the fine arts are dwelt on with much innocent pleasure. They thrum a few tunes on the piano, and the whole family listen and approve. All unite in singing, in a somewhat discordant and uncultured manner, a few psalm-tunes or songs, and take more comfort in them than many amateurs do in their well-executed performances.

So goes the world with the Daytons; and when you visit them, if you often feel that you could ask more and suggest much improvement, yet you cannot help enjoying the quiet satisfaction which breathes around you.

Now right across the way from the Daytons live the Mores; and the Mores are the very opposites of the Daytons.

Everything about their establishment is brought to the highest point of culture. The carriage-drive never shows a weed, the lawn is velvet, the flower-beds ever blooming, the fruit-trees and vines grow exactly like the patterns in the best pomological treatises. Within doors the housekeeping is faultless,—all seems to be moving in time and tune,—the table is more than good, it is superlative,—every article is in its way a model,—the children appear to you to be growing up after the most patent-right method, duly trained, snipped, and cultured, like the pear-trees, and grape-vines. Nothing is left to accident, or done without much laborious consideration of the best manner of doing it; and the consequences, in the eyes of their simple unsophisticated neighbours, are very wonderful.

Nevertheless, this is not a happy family. All their perfections do not begin to afford them one tithe of the satisfaction that the Daytons derive from their ragged and scrambling performances.

The two daughters, Jane and Maria, had naturally very sweet voices, and when they were little, trilled tunes in a very pleasant and bird-like manner. But now, having been instructed by the best masters, and heard the very first artists, they never sing or play; the piano is shut, and their voices are dumb. If you request a song, they tell you that they never sing now; papa has such an exquisite taste, he takes no interest in any common music; in short, having heard Jenny Lind, Grisi, Alboni, Mario, and others of the tuneful shell, this family have concluded to abide in silence. As to any music that *they* could make, it isn't to be thought of.

For the same reason, the daughters, after attending, for a quarter or two, the drawing exercises of a celebrated teacher, threw up their pencils in disgust, and tore up very pretty and agreeable sketches which were the marvel of their good-natured, admiring neighbours. If they could draw like Signor Scratchalini, if they could hope to become perfect artists, they tell you they would have persevered; but they have taken lessons enough to learn that drawing is the labour of a life-time, and, not having a life-time to give to it, they resolve to do nothing at all.

They have also, for a similar reason, given up letter-writing. If their chirography were as elegant as Charlotte Cushman's,—if they were perfect mistresses of polite English,—if they were gifted with wit, humour, and fancy, like the first masters of style,—they would take pleasure in epistolary composition, and be good correspondents; but anything short of that is so intolerable, that, except in cases of life and death or urgent business, you cannot get a line out of them. Yet they write very fair, agreeable, womanly letters, and would write much better ones, if they allowed themselves a little more practice.

Mrs. More is devoured by care. She sits with a clouded brow in her elegant, well-regulated house; and when you talk with her, you are surprised to learn that everything in it is in the most dreadful disorder from one end to the other. You ask for particulars, and find that the disorder has relation to exquisite standards of the ways of doing things, derived from observation of life in the most subdivided state of European service,—to all of which she has not as yet been able to raise her domestics. You compliment her on her cook, and she responds, in plaintive accents, "She can do a few things decently, but she is nothing of a cook." You refer with enthusiasm to her bread, her coffee, her muffins and hot rolls, and she listens and sighs. "Yes," she admits, "these are eatable,—not bad; but you should have seen the rolls at a certain *café* in Paris, and the bread at a certain nobleman's in England, where they had a bakery in the castle, and a French baker, who did nothing at all but refine and perfect the idea of bread. When she thinks of these things, everything in comparison is so coarse and rough!—but then she has learned to be comfortable." Thus, in every department of housekeeping, to this too-well instructed person,

"Hills peep o'er hills, and Alps on Alps arise."

Not a thing in her wide and apparently beautifully-kept establishment is ever done well enough to elicit from her more than a sigh of toleration. "I suppose it must do," she faintly breathes, when poor human nature, having tried and tried again, evidently has got to the boundaries of its capabilities; "you may let it go, Jane; I never expect to be suited."

The poor woman, in the midst of possessions and attainments which excite the envy of her neighbours, is utterly restless and wretched, and feels herself always baffled and unsuccessful. Her exacting nature makes her dissatisfied with herself in everything that she undertakes, and equally dissatisfied with others. In the whole family there is little of that pleasure which comes from the consciousness of mutual admiration and esteem, because each one is pitched to so exquisite a tone that each is afraid to touch another for fear of making discord. They are afraid of each other everywhere. They cannot sing to each other, play to each other, write to each other; they cannot even converse together with any freedom, because each knows that the others are so dismally well-informed and critically instructed.

Though all agree in a secret contempt for their neighbours over the way, as living in a most heathenish state of ignorant contentment, yet it is a fact that the elegant brother John will often, on the sly, slip into the Daytons' to spend an evening, and join them in singing glees and catches to their old rattling piano, and have a jolly time of it, which he remembers in contrast with the dull, silent hours at home. Kate Dayton has an uncultivated voice, which often falls from pitch; but she has a perfectly infectious gaiety of good nature, and when she is once at the piano, and all join in some merry troll, he begins to think that there may be something better even than good singing; and then they have dances and charades and games, all in such contented, jolly, *impromptu* ignorance of the unities of time, place, and circumstance, that he sometimes doubts, where ignorance is such bliss, whether it isn't in truth folly to be wise.

Jane and Maria laugh at John for his partiality to the Daytons, and yet they themselves feel the same attraction. At the Daytons' they, somehow, find themselves heroines; their drawings are so admired, their singing is so charming to these uncultured ears, that they are often beguiled into giving pleasure with their own despised acquirements; and Jane, somehow, is very tolerant of the devoted attention of Will Dayton, a joyous, honest-hearted fellow, whom, in her heart of hearts, she likes none the worse for being unexacting and simple enough to think her a wonder of taste and accomplishments. Will, of course, is the furthest possible from the Admirable Crichtons and exquisite Sir Philip Sidneys whom Mrs. More and the young ladies talk up at their leisure, and adorn with feathers from every royal and celestial bird, when they are discussing ideal, possible husbands. He is not in any way distinguished, except for a kind heart, strong native good sense, and a manly energy that has carried him straight into the very heart of many a citadel of life, before which the superior and more refined Mr. John had set himself down to deliberate upon the best and most elegant way of taking it. Will's plain, homely intelligence has often in five minutes disentangled some ethereal snarl in which these exquisite Mores had spun themselves up, and brought them to his own way of thinking by that sort of disenchanting process which honest, practical sense sometimes exerts over ideality.

The fact is, however, that in each of these families there is a natural defect, which requires something from the other to remedy it. Taking happiness as the standard, the Daytons have it as against the Mores. Taking attainment as the standard, the Mores have it as against the Daytons. A portion of the discontented ideality of the Mores would stimulate the Daytons to refine and perfect many things which might easily be made better, did they care enough to have them so; and a portion of the Daytons' self-satisfied contentment would make the attainments and refinements of the Mores of some practical use in advancing their own happiness.

But between these two classes of natures lies another, to which has been given an equal share of ideality,—in which the conception and the desire of excellence are equally strong, but in which a discriminating common sense acts like a balance-wheel in machinery. What is the reason that the most exacting idealists never make themselves unhappy about not being able to fly like a bird or swim like a fish? Because common sense teaches them that these accomplishments are so utterly out of the question, that they never arise to the mind as objects of desire. In these well-balanced minds we speak of, common-sense runs an instinctive line all through life between the attainable and the unattainable, and sets the key of desire accordingly.

Common sense teaches that there is no one branch of human art or science in which perfection is not a point for ever receding. A botanist gravely assures us that to become perfect in the knowledge of one branch of sea-weeds would take all the time and strength of a man for a life-time. There is no limit to music, to the fine arts. There is never a time when the gardener can rest, saying that his garden is perfect. Housekeeping, cooking, sewing, knitting, may all, for aught we know, be pushed on for ever, without exhausting the capabilities for doing better.

But while attainment in everything is endless, circumstances forbid the greater part of human beings attaining, in any direction, the half of what they see would be desirable; and the difference between the miserable idealist and the contented realist often is not that both do not see what needs to be done for perfection, but that, seeing it, one is satisfied with the attainable, and the other for ever frets and wears himself out on the unattainable.

The principal of a large and complicated public institution was complimented on maintaining such uniformity of cheerfulness amid such a diversity of cares. "I've made up my mind to be satisfied, when things are done *half* as well as I would have them," was his answer, and the same philosophy would apply with cheering results to the domestic sphere.

There is a saying which one often hears among common people, that such and such a one are persons who never could be happy, unless everything went "*just so*,"—that is, in accordance with their highest conceptions.

When these persons are women, and undertake the sway of a home empire, they are sure to be miserable, and to make others so; for home is a place where, by no kind of magic possible to woman, can everything be always made to go "just so."

We may read treatises on education,—and very excellent ones there are. We may read very nice stories illustrating home management, in which book-children and book-servants all work into the author's plan with obliging unanimity; but every real child and real servant is an uncompromising fact, whose working into our ideal of life cannot be predicted with any degree of certainty. A husband is another absolute fact, of whose conformity to any ideal conceptions no positive account can be given. So, when a person has the most charming theories of education, the most complete ideals of life, it is often his lot to sit bound hand and foot, and see them all trampled under the heel of opposing circumstances.

Nothing is easier than to make an ideal garden. We lay out our grounds, dig, plant, transplant, manure.

We read catalogues of roses till we are bewildered with their lustrous glories. We set our plum, pear, and peach; we luxuriate, in advance, on bushels of choicest grapes, and our theoretic garden is Paradise Regained. But in the actual garden there are cut worms for every cabbage, squash-bugs for all the melons, slugs and rose-bugs for the roses, curculios for the plums, fire-blight for pears, yellows for peaches, mildew for grapes, and late and early frosts, droughts, winds, and hail-storms here and there for all.

The garden and the family are fair pictures of each other. Both are capable of the most ravishing representations on paper; and the rules and directions for creating beauty and perfection in both, can be made so apparently plain that he who runneth may read, and it would seem that a fool need not err therein; and yet the actual results are always halting miles away behind expectation and desire.

It would be an incalculable gain to domestic happiness, if people would begin the concert of life with their instruments tuned to a very low pitch: they who receive the most happiness are generally they who demand and expect the least.

Ideality often becomes an insidious mental and moral disease, acting all the more subtly from its alliances with what is highest and noblest within us. Shall we not aspire to be perfect? Shall we be content with low measures and low standards in anything? To these inquiries there seems of course to be but one answer; yet the individual driven forward in blind, unreasoning aspiration, becomes wearied, bewildered, discontented, restless, fretful, and miserable.

An unhappy person can never make others happy. The creators and governors of a home, who are themselves restless and inharmonious, cannot make harmony and peace. This is the secret reason why many a pure, good, conscientious person is only a source of uneasiness in family-life. They are exacting, discontented, unhappy; and spread the discontent and unhappiness about them. They are, to begin with, on poor terms with themselves; they do not like themselves; they do not like their own appearance, manners, education, accomplishments; on all these points they try themselves by ideal standards, and find themselves wanting. In morals, in religion, too, the same introverted scrutiny detects only errors and evils, till all life seems to them a miserable, hopeless failure, and they wish they had never been born. They are angry and disgusted with themselves; there is no self-toleration or self-endurance. And persons in a chronic quarrel with themselves are very apt to quarrel with others. That exacting nature which has no patience with one's own inevitable frailties and errors has none for those of others; and thus the great motive by which Christianity enforces tolerance of the faults of others, loses its hold. There are people who make no allowances either for themselves or anybody else, but are equally angry and disgusted with both.

Now it is important that those finely-strung natures in which ideality largely predominates should begin life by a religious care and restraint of this faculty. As the case often stands, however, religion only intensifies the difficulty, by adding stringency to exaction and censoriousness, driving the subject up with an unremitting strain, till the very cords of reason sometimes snap. Yet, properly understood and used, religion is the only cure for the evil of diseased ideality. The Christian religion is the only one that ever proposed to give to all human beings, however various the range of their nature and desires, the great underlying gift of *rest*. Its Author, with a strength of assurance which only supreme divinity can justify, promises *rest* to all persons, under all circumstances, with all sorts of natures, all sorts of wants, and all sorts of defects. The invitation is as wide as the human race: "Come unto me, all ye that labour and are heavy-laden, and I will give you REST."

Now this is the more remarkable, as this gracious promise is accompanied by the presentation of a standard of perfection which is more ideal and exacting than any other that has ever been placed before mankind,—which, in so many words, sets up absolute perfection as the only true goal of aspiration.

The problem which Jesus proposes to human nature is endless aspiration steadied by endless peace,—a perfectly restful, yet unceasing effort after a good which is never to be attained till we attain a higher and more perfect form of existence. It is because this problem is insolvable by any human wisdom, that He says that they who take His yoke upon them must learn of Him, for He alone can make the perfect yoke easy, and its burden light.

The first lesson in this benignant school must lie like a strong, broad foundation under every structure on which we wish to rear a happy life,—and that is, that the full gratification of the faculty of ideality is never to be expected in this present stage of existence, but is to be transferred to a future life. Ideality, with its incessant, restless longings and yearnings, is snubbed and turned out of doors by human philosophy, when philosophy becomes middle-aged and sulky with repeated disappointments,—it is be-rated as a cheat and a liar,—told to hold its tongue and take itself elsewhere; but Christianity bids it be of good cheer, still to aspire and hope and prophesy, and points to a future where all its dreams shall be outdone by reality.

A full faith in such a perfect future—a perfect faith that God has planted in man no desire which he cannot train to complete enjoyment in that future—gives the mind rest and contentment to postpone for a while gratifications that will certainly come at last.

Such a faith is better even than that native philosophical good sense which restrains the ideal calculations and hopes of some; for it has a wider scope and a deeper power.

We have seen, in our time, a woman gifted with all those faculties which rejoice in the refinements of society, dispensing the elegant hospitalities of a bountiful home—joyful and giving joy. A sudden reverse has swept all this away; the wealth on which it was based has melted like a fog-bank in a warm morning, and we have seen her with her little family beginning life again in the log-cabin of a Western settlement. We have seen her sitting in the door of the one room that took the place of parlour, bed-room, and nursery, cheerfully making her children's morning toilette by the help of the one tin wash-bowl that takes the place of her well-arranged bathing and dressing-rooms; and yet, as she twined their curls over her fingers, she had a laugh and a jest and cheerful word for all. The few morning-glories that she was training over her rude porch seemed as much a source of delight to her as her former green-house and garden; and the adjustment of the one or two shelves whereon were the half-dozen books left of the library, her husband's private papers, and her own and her children's wardrobes, was entered into daily with a zealous interest as if she had never known a wider sphere.

Such facility of accommodation to life's reverses is sometimes supposed to be merely the result of a hopeful and cheerful temperament; in this case it was purely the work of religion. In early life, this same woman had been the discontented slave of ideality, had sighed with vain longings in the midst of real and substantial comfort, had felt even the creasing of the rose-leaves of her pillow an intolerable annoyance. Now she has resigned herself to the work and toil of life as the soldier does to the duties of the camp, satisfied to do and to bear, enjoying with a free heart the small daily pleasures which spring up like wild-flowers amid daily toils and annoyances, and looking to the end of the campaign for rest and congenial scenes.

This woman has within her the powers and gifts of an artist; but her pencils and her colours are resolutely laid away, and she sits hour after hour darning her children's stockings, and turning and arranging a scanty wardrobe which no ingenuity can make more than decent. She was a beautiful musician; but a musical instrument is now a thing of the past; she only lulls her baby to sleep with snatches of the songs which used to form the attraction of brilliant *salons*. She feels that a world of tastes and talents are lying dormant in her while she is doing the daily work of a nurse, cook, and seamstress; but she remembers WHO took upon Him the form of a servant before her, and she has full faith that her beautiful gifts, like bulbs sleeping under ground, shall come up and blossom again in that fair future which He has promised. Therefore it is that she has no sighs for the present or the past,—no quarrel with her life, or her lot in it; she is in harmony with herself and with all around her; her husband looks upon her as a fair daily miracle, and her children rise up and call her blessed.

But, having laid the broad foundation of faith in a better life, as the basis on which to ground our present happiness, we who are of the ideal nature must proceed to build thereon wisely.

In the first place, we must cultivate the duty of *self*-patience and *self*-toleration. Of all the religionists and moralists who ever taught, Fénelon is the only one who has distinctly formulated the duty which a self-educator owes to himself. HAVE PATIENCE WITH YOURSELF is a direction often occurring in his writings, and a most important one it is,—because patience with ourselves is essential if we would have patience with others. Let us look through the world. Who are the people easiest to be pleased, most sunny, most urbane, most tolerant? Are they not persons, from constitution and temperament, on good terms with themselves,—people who do not ask much of themselves or try themselves severely, and who, therefore, are in a good humour for looking upon others? But how is a person who is conscious of a hundred daily faults and errors to have patience with himself? The question may be answered by asking, What would you say to a child who fretted, scolded, dashed down his slate, and threw his book on the floor, because he made mistakes in his arithmetic? You would say, of course, "You are but a learner; it is not to be expected that you will not make mistakes; all children do. Have patience." Just as you would talk to that child, talk to yourself. Be reconciled to a lot of inevitable imperfection; be content to try continually, and often to fail. It is the inevitable condition of human existence, and is to be accepted as such. A patient acceptance of mortifications and of defeats of our life's labour is often more efficacious for our moral advancement than even our victories.

In the next place, we must school ourselves not to look with restless desire to degrees of excellence in any department of life which circumstances evidently forbid our attaining. For a woman with plenty of money and plenty of well-trained servants to be content to have fly-specked windows, or littered rooms, or a slovenly-ordered table, is a sin. But in a woman in feeble health, encumbered with a flock of restless little ones, and whose circumstances allow her to keep but one servant, it may be a piece of moral heroism to shut her eyes on many such things, while securing mere essentials to life and health. It may be a virtue in her not to push neatness to such lengths as to wear herself out, or to break down her only servant, and to be resigned to have her tastes and preferences for order, cleanliness, and beauty crossed, as she would resign herself to any other affliction. No purgatory can be more severe to people of a thorough and exact nature than to be so situated that they can only half do everything they undertake; yet such is the fiery trial to which many a one is subjected. Life seems to drive them along without giving them time for anything; everything is a ragged, hasty performance, of which the mind most keenly sees and feels the raggedness and hastiness. Even one thing done as it really ought to be done, would be a rest and refreshment to the soul; but nowhere, in any department of its undertakings, is there any such thing to be perceived.

But there are cases where a great deal of wear and tear can be saved to the nerves by a considerate making up of one's mind as to how much, in certain circumstances, had better be undertaken at all. Let the circumstances of life be surveyed, the objects we are pursuing arranged and counted, and see if there are not things here and there that may be thrown out of our plans entirely, that others may be better executed.

What if the whole care of expensive table luxuries, like cake and preserves, be thrown out of a housekeeper's budget, in order that the essential articles of cookery may be better prepared? What if ruffling, embroidery, and the entire department of kindred fine arts be thrown out of her calculations in providing for the clothing of a family? Many a feeble woman has died of too much ruffling, as she patiently sat up night after night sewing the thread of a precious, invaluable life into elaborate articles which her children were none the healthier or more virtuous for wearing.

Ideality is constantly ramifying and extending the department of the toilette and the needle into a world of work and worry, wherein distracted women wander up and down, seeing no end anywhere. The sewing-machine was announced as a relief to these toils; but has it proved so? We trow not. It only amounts to this,—that now there can be seventy-two tucks on each little petticoat, instead of fifteen, as before, and that twice as many garments are made up and held to be necessary as formerly. The women still sew to the limit of human endurance; and still the old proverb holds good, that woman's work is never done.

In the matter of dress, much wear and tear of spirit and nerves may be saved by not beginning to go in certain directions, well knowing that they will take us beyond our resources of time, strength, and money.

There is one word of fear in the vocabulary of the

women of our time, which must be pondered advisedly, —TRIMMING. In old times a good garment was enough; now-a-days a garment is nothing without trimming. Everything, from the first article that the baby wears up to the elaborate dress of the bride, must be trimmed at a rate that makes the trimming more than the original article. A dress can be made in a day, but it cannot be trimmed under two or three days. Let a faithful, conscientious woman make up her mind how much of all this burden of life she will assume, remembering wisely that there is no end to ideality in anything, and that the only way to deal with many perplexing parts of life is to leave them out altogether.

Mrs. Kirkland, in her very amusing account of her log-cabin experiences, tells us of the great disquiet and inconvenience she had in attempting to arrange in her lowly abode, a most convenient clothes-press, which was manifestly too large for the establishment. Having laboured with the cumbersome convenience for a great length of time, and with much discomfort, she at last resigned the ordering of it to a brawny-armed damsel of the forest, who began by pitching it out of doors, with the comprehensive remark, that, "where there wasn't room for a thing, there wasn't."

The wisdom which inspired the remark of this rustic maiden might have saved the lives of many matrons, who have worn themselves out in vain attempts to make comforts and conveniences out of things which they had better have thrown out of doors altogether.

True, it requires some judgment to know what, among objects commonly pursued in any department, we really ought to reject; and it requires independence and steadiness to say, "I will not begin to try to do certain things that others are doing, and that, perhaps, they expect of me;" but there comes great leisure and quietness of spirit from the gaps thus made. When the unwieldy clothes-press was once cast out, everything in the log-cabin could have room.

A mother, who is anxiously trying to reconcile the watchful care and training of her little ones with the maintenance of fashionable calls and parties, may lose her life in the effort to do both, and do both in so imperfect a manner as never to give her a moment's peace. But on the morrow after she comes to the serious and Christian resolve, "The training of my children is all that I *can* do well, and henceforth it shall be my *sole* object," there falls into her tumultuous life a Sabbath pause of peace and leisure. It is true that she is still doing a work in which absolute perfection ever recedes; but she can make relative attainments far nearer the standard than before.

Lastly, under the head of ideality, let us resolve to be satisfied with our own past doings, when at the time of doing we used all the light God gave us and did all in our power.

The backward action of ideality is often full as tormenting as its forward and prospective movements. The moment a thing is done and over, one would think that good sense would lead us to drop it like a stone into the ocean; but the morbid idealist cannot cut loose from the past.

"Was that, after all, the *best* thing? Would it not have been better so or so?" And the self-tormented individual lies wakeful, during weary night-hours, revolving a thousand possibilities, and conjuring up a thousand vague perhapses. "If I had only done so, now, perhaps this result would have followed, or that would not;" and as there is never any saying but that so it might have turned out, the labyrinth and the discontent are alike endless.

Now there is grand good sense in the Apostle's direction, "Forgetting the things that are behind, press forward." The idealist should charge himself, as with an oath of God, to let the past alone as an accomplished fact, solely concerning himself with the inquiry, "Did I not do the best I *then* knew how?"

The maxim of the Quietists is, that, when we have acted according to the best light we have, we have expressed the will of God under those circumstances,—since, had it been otherwise, more and different light would have been given us; and with the will of God done by ourselves as by Himself, it is our duty to be content.

Having written thus far in my article, and finding nothing more at hand to add to it, I went into the parlour to read it to Jennie and Mrs. Crowfield. I found the former engaged in the task of binding sixty yards of quilling, (so I think she called it,) which were absolutely necessary for perfecting a dress: and the latter was braiding one of seven little petticoats, stamped with elaborate patterns, which she had taken from Marianne, because that virtuous matron was ruining her eyes and health in a blind push to get them done before October.

Both approved and admired my piece, and I thought of Saint Anthony's preaching to the fishes:—

> "The sermon once ended,
> The good man descended,
> And the pikes went on stealing.
> The eels went on eeling,
> The crabs were backsliders,
> The stockfish thick-siders:
> Much delighted were they,
> But went on their own way."

THE END.